Salt

in an

Unsavory World

One Person Can Make a Difference

Janet A. Nicolet

Salt in an Unsavory World

Copyright 2013 © by Janet A. Nicolet

©**All rights reserved.** No part of this book may be reproduced, stored in a retrievable system, or transmitted in any form or by any means without the prior written permission of the publisher or author, except in the case of brief quotations in articles and reviews.

First Printing

Cover designed by:
    Tara Martinez, Digital Design Student
    Haney Technical Center, Lynn Haven, Florida

All characters and events portrayed are fictitious and any resemblance to incidents, or persons, living or dead, are purely coincidental. Any interaction with the characters is purely fiction.

All Scripture quotations are taken from the King James Version of the Bible.

ISBN: 978-1-84961-184-8
Published by: RealTime Publishing – Limerick, Ireland
Printed in the United States of America and Europe

Acknowledgements

When writing a book, editors and contributors are two groups of people who are a must. They are invaluable with their time, knowledge and skill. I am grateful to the following people who have been my right hand since the beginning of this project:

Editors:
- Teri French
- Dave Hanson
- Jean Mallory
- Bernice Riley
- Al Tidwell

Contributors:
- Jason Heath
- Jason Jeter
- Paul Major

I would also like to thank my family and friends who have encouraged me to write another book. Without their nudging - and at my age, I would probably be sitting back in my recliner watching the world goes by.

Dedication

I want to dedicate this writing and also commend those volunteers who give of themselves with their selfless service to programs which provide assistance for the staggering number of neglected and abused children in our country. They make a positive difference in the life of a child.

Janet A. Nicolet

SALT

*In the Lord's teachings it is symbolic
of that spiritual health and vigour
essential to Christian virtue . . .
and
<u>counteractive</u> of the corruption
that is in the world.*

---

*From Vine's Expository Dictionary
Of the Old and New Testament Words
1981- Fleming H. Revell Company
Old Tappan, New Jersey*

Foreword

I am pleased that Janet has drawn attention to the plight of neglected and abused children through her writing. Most people have no idea that 1 out of every 4 girls is abused and 1 out of every 6 boys, almost always by someone they know. The statistics for domestic violence are astounding.

All it takes to make a difference in a child's life is the desire to do so. Life's experiences are more valuable than any college degree. Anyone who cheers for the underdog is a contender for the CASA/GAL type of volunteerism.

As a CASA (Court Appointed Special Advocate), I can speak for the child in court because I have spoken with the child and/or feel certain that I can convey what is in the child's best interest. My written testimony to the judge is factual and is relied upon to be so. I do make a difference.

Teri French,
Advocate and Board Member of CASA Monroe,
Madisonville, TN

Janet A. Nicolet

Chapter 1

Velma Pearce – 'Grandma Pearce' to most folks in Middleton, Washington - reached the pavement from the last step of the bus and raised her umbrella. Rain did not deter her or the other residents in the area from their daily routine, as it was a normal weather pattern for that time of year.

It was Monday, the third day of October. With her social security check in the bank and her shopping list in her hand, she made her way to the grocery store's entrance.

"Mornin', Ms. Pearce," said a young female clerk standing behind the checkout counter.

"Good morning," came her cheery reply with an added smile. "How's that baby girl of yours?"

"Just fine, thank you. She's a real bundle of joy."

"Wonderful!"

As Velma talked, she reached for one of the plastic sleeves provided for her wet umbrella.

She then tugged at the shopping cart to dislodge it from the others that were stacked in line, but it wouldn't come free. Then she gave it a good yank, but it still would not budge. A bag-boy saw her dilemma and stepped over to help her.

"Thank you, son."

"You're welcome, ma'am."

Her list of items was not very long, since she could not carry heavy shopping bags. At eighty-years-*young* and a widow, her kids and grandkids had tried on numerous occasions to take her shopping, but she kindly refused them. She wanted to still fend for herself as long as she could.

Velma had stopped driving her car a year ago when she began having trouble with her eyes. Even after the cataracts were removed from both eyes, she still had a problem focusing. It did not deter her from going wherever she wanted or had to go – by bus, that is.

She would not have to buy many vegetables, as having grown up on a farm she still grew her own on a small plot of land next to her house. As her grandchildren grew up they would come over to her place with their parents after school or on Saturdays to pick peas from the vines and dig up carrots, turnips, rutabagas and potatoes. Velma froze most of her vegetables and would also provide her neighbors with a hefty bag of an assortment of vegetables.

To those who would question her need for a garden, she would quip, "You can take the lady out of the farm, but you can't take the farm out of the lady." Then she would grin.

The large freezer in her house also held a portion of a side of beef and pork. Velma and her son, Stephen, together made that yearly purchase from a local farmer who had been a close friend of the Pearce family. Therefore, her shopping list was quite brief.

The few things on her list would not keep her in the store for long. Velma had a scheduled appointment with a young fourth-grader at the child's foster parents' home. She had been a long-time volunteer as a Court Appointed Special Advocate (CASA) for abused and neglected children in her county. Her plan that morning was to take the groceries home, fix a bite to eat and then catch the bus that would take her across town for her visit with the young girl.

As she passed people in the aisles, she nodded and smiled. Some returned her courteous greeting, while others ignored her, thinking, *I don't know her* or *who's that ol' lady smiling at?* It was obvious by their facial expressions what they were thinking.

Not the same old Middleton, Velma thought. *People aren't as friendly anymore.* But she quickly sloughed off that negative thought, not allowing it to take away her always-present enjoyment of life.

Velma finished her shopping and headed out the automatic door with her umbrella and purse in one hand and the two bags of groceries in the other hand. *Glad it quit raining* she thought, as she maneuvered around a puddle of water.

She walked slowly because recently, her right hip bothered her. She had endured for longer than she could remember a dull aching pain that came and went in her thigh area. In three weeks, that would be taken care of with a hip replacement. "Oh, to be free of this pain," she would often say aloud when she climbed into bed after a day of coping with more pain than usual.

Ever so slowly, she made her way to the bus stop, but would stop a couple of times to take a deep breath and then continued on. She stepped onto the sidewalk from the black-topped parking lot and took a fleeting glance to the left to check for her bus, and in so doing leaned her right shoulder out a little toward the street. She could not have imagined what would happen to her in the next couple of seconds.

When Velma leaned out - as quick as the blink of an eye - she was hit and tossed to the ground by the handlebar of a bicycle ridden by a thirteen-year-old boy. The handlebar of the bike had caught her right elbow, twisting her around and down to the ground. Her groceries went flying everywhere.

The boy on the bicycle also fell to the ground, but quickly made his way to his feet. He got down on one knee and leaned over Velma, who at that point was lying face down. Her head was in the dirt alongside the sidewalk where a hedge ran the length of the parking lot.

He touched the sleeve of her coat, "Lady? Lady? Are you okay?" When she did not respond, he closed his eyes and gasped, "Oh, please lady – tell me you're all right."

No sound came from the woman as she lay prostrate on the ground.

He shook his head *oh, no -- I think she's dead?* He was frightened out of his wits. *I can't believe I did this. What's my mom going to say?* He stood up and looked around with the hope of seeing an adult standing close by, but not so. He paced back and forth, wondering what he should do. Out of the clear blue he heard the words, "Call 9-1-1." He looked around but saw no one, and in dismay shook his head to clear his thoughts. Even so, he reached into his pocket to retrieve his cell phone.

On the day he received the phone his mom had said, "Son, put 9-1-1 in your cell phone under just the letter A. That will make it the first number you come to when you're in a hurry to make an emergency call." He was so glad that for once he had listened to her.

"9-1-1, what is your emergency?" asked the female voice on the other end of the line.

"Um . . . I . . . I . . . ah, need help."

"What kind of help?"

"For a lady. I knocked her down with my bike and I don't know what to do."

"Where are you?"

"In front of the Safeway store on Alexander Street. I don't know the address."

"That's okay. Is she awake?"

"No," he said, in a desperate tone.

"What's your name?"

"Tony."

"Tony what?"

"Tony Ramirez."

"How old are you, Tony?"

"Thirteen."

He continued to answer all the many questions that were asked of him.

"Help is on the way, Tony. Stay with her and try to comfort her, but please, please do not move her."

"I won't. Thank you." He had no sooner pushed the 'off' button on his phone when he heard a siren blaring in the distance. His heart was pounding a mile-a-minute as he knelt down beside Mrs. Pearce. "Lady, an ambulance is coming. I'm so sorry that I hurt you. Please forgive me. I'm so sorry."

Mrs. Pearce did not answer, nor did she stir. The ambulance pulled into the driveway of the grocery store to get out of traffic. Two men hopped out and began taking equipment out of the rear of the ambulance. They were at her side in no time. Seconds later, a squad car pulled into the driveway and two policemen made their way to the scene.

Tony stood anxiously by, hands in his pockets, his head turning from one person to another as they attended to Mrs. Pearce. *I should call my mother, but I don't want to scare her. What'll I do?* Just then one of the policemen approached him.

Pointing to the bike that lay on the ground, Sergeant Jackson, the lead policeman asked, "Is that your bike, son?"

"Yesss, sir," Tony responded.

"So, tell me what happened?"

Ashamed to face the police officer, Tony stared at the ground. "I was, ah . . . um . . . I was riding along on the sidewalk, and um, I ah . . . oh, gosh, it happened so fast, I really don't know how I did it."

"Slow down. I'm interested in just the facts. Which way were you traveling?"

Pointing to his left, "That way."

"Okay. Did you see the lady?"

"Yes. But, I didn't think I was that close to her. I'm sorry. I didn't mean to hurt her."

"I know. I know, son. Just take it easy. I need you to give me your address and phone number."

Tony reluctantly gave him that information, thinking that he now would be in the police files as a bad person - forever.

After the attendants placed a neck brace on Mrs. Pearce, she was then carefully placed on a gurney and into the ambulance. Within a minute or so, the siren began wailing as the driver turned the ambulance around to head back out of the driveway. Tony stood there shaking his head slowly from side to side and muttering, "If she's dead, I'm going to prison."

"Come on, son. We're taking you home," said the police officer.

The rookie policeman picked up the damaged bicycle and mirror parts that were strewn around on the sidewalk, putting them into the trunk of the squad car.

"Tony, did you hear me, I said get into the car," came the gentle but yet stern command of Sgt. Jackson.

Tony stood there mortified by what he had just done.

Chapter 2

Velma had continued to stroll along the beach each day after her husband's death; something the two had enjoyed doing after George's retirement. They had sometimes held hands, appreciating and savoring that special time together. During the winter though, their hands were tucked deep down into their coat pockets, their collars turned up and their shoulders hunched forward as they braced themselves against the cold winter wind as it whipped across the waters of the Pacific. The walk, in whatever weather, was so invigorating as well as good exercise for their aging bodies. "Look, Velma!" catching his wife's attention, George would point down to the small hole in the sand where a clam had burrowed itself. "We should've brought along a bucket and shovel and got us a mess of clams for tonight's dinner."

Sometimes the two would look for unusual pieces of driftwood. George loved to spend time in his workshop where he would take a piece of that driftwood and craft it into a lamp or some other piece of art work.

Velma (Scott) Pearce had lived in Middleton all her life. She was born in a farmhouse just outside of town, as were her six siblings. In the early 1920s, her dad had bought the farm with money left to him by his deceased parents. He got a good deal on the place, since the owners were elderly and could not work the land any longer.

He raised strawberries in the spring and summer and harvested squash and pumpkins later in the year. He sold the produce at the farmer's market in town, which was located on the busy main two-lane dirt road that ran north and south just off the Pacific Ocean. Her mother took in ironing from well-to-do families who summered along the coast.

Middleton was so named by its founding fathers because it is located half-way between the northern and southern borders of the State of Washington and smack in the middle of the coastline of Grays Harbor County. It was quite a small town back then, with a population of three-hundred and thirty-seven – so noted in the 1920 census. It would grow exponentially to become a noteworthy city in the early '50s when a manufacturing plant moved into the area just east of the city. It was a fifteen-minute drive to work for the employees, but they did not care, as the job provided a good living for their families. The company settled into that area, due to shipping accessibility on State Road 109 that runs along the Pacific coast and also with the railroad that passes through the area.

The farm helped the family to be self-sustaining. Mr. Scott had a few head of cattle, a couple of milk cows and generally kept two pigs which he butchered and sold each year. He also had a whole henhouse full of chickens that provided plenty of eggs for the family and to sell.

They raised four boys and three girls; all of them had a list of chores to perform when they got home from school each day and on weekends. The girls were given the task of collecting eggs and they also had to help their mother make soap. That was a long and arduous process, where Mrs. Scott would use a mixture of lard and a potash solution from wood ashes. The fat was first melted and strained and then the potash solution stirred into the hot fat. Continuous stirring during both procedures was important, and that's where the Scott girls were a big help, even though it was a tedious job.

The boys were taught at an early age to drive the tractor, in order to haul the fruit back in a wagon to the collection area near the barn. The loading and unloading was quite time consuming. Feeding of the livestock also fell into their capable hands.

Summers were spent with both the boys and girls picking strawberries and hoeing or retrieving vegetables from a huge garden. Everyone helped in the fall with the squash and pumpkins. They so enjoyed those times when neighbors were invited in October and November to come in and select their own pumpkins for a nickel each and ten cents for the extra-large ones.

Velma was a pretty girl right from birth. She was the youngest child and favored by her dad, who called her *my lil wiggle-worm* because she could not sit still. Her brothers used to say in a terse manner and with wrinkled noses, "She's a daddy's girl." By one of her sisters she was known as *Goodie-Two-Shoes*. That label stuck with her for years because she was a very obedient child, who especially did not like to lie. There were times when her siblings misbehaved and they wanted her to lie to their parents in order to keep themselves out of trouble – but she would refuse. As she reached her teens, she also had a knack for being able to defuse arguments between siblings and friends. She just had a winning way about her with most folks.

The Scott family attended a very small church a half-mile from the farm, where Velma's dad taught the adult Sunday school class, which on most Sundays consisted of ten to twelve individuals.

At home, Mr. Scott was adamant about everyone attending the family prayer time each evening before the children retired for the night. It was not always the favorite time for some of the children, especially if they had something else they *really* wanted to do. Velma relished that time when all the kids sat on the large round handmade rug as their father read a Bible scripture and then led them in prayer. She loved the togetherness of that family time.

That colorful braided rug covered most of the area in front of the fireplace. Their mother, along with some ladies from the church had made that floor covering soon after the young newlyweds had moved into the farmhouse. It became a favorite possession of Mrs. Scott. She beamed with pride whenever a visitor complimented her on its beauty. Velma sought possession of it when her mother passed away. It now adorns the area right in front of her fireplace.

George Pearce had returned home in late-1945, after fighting the Japanese on the island of Okinawa during WWII and resumed his relationship with Velma, his childhood sweetheart. She was on his mind day and night during his time on the battlefield. She kept his sanity intact in the midst of the long days and nights in the heat, humidity and gunfire.

The two spent that next year getting reacquainted while she completed courses she was taking at a vocational-technical school in the next city. George and Velma married in 1946.

In 1947, a post-war housing area was built in Middleton, which became occupied with mostly local men who had returned from war to marry the local women. George and Velma would move into one of those adorable small white two-bedroom bungalows just after their second wedding anniversary.

Those years after WWII has been called the baby-boom era, to which the couple took seriously. Within the next ten years they had six children, four boys and two girls. There would have been a seventh child, but that baby girl was still-born. It was a heartache that took quite some time for both George and Velma to recover from. The two girls were very disappointed, too, as the boys in the family had always outnumbered the girls, and they were hoping for a sister to boost their number.

George worked as an automobile mechanic at a local garage at first, but later hired on at the new manufacturing company in the area. He would retire years later from that same company as a supervisor in shipping and receiving.

They had moved after their third child was born, from the cute little white bungalow to a much larger four-bedroom home on a two-acre plot of land that overlooked the Pacific Ocean. It was a serene location, which brought great peace to both George and Velma in the chaotic, but still very enjoyable world they lived in with six children.

They relished that quietude even more after the children had grown and left home.

Out on the back veranda, which ran the width of the house, the two would sit in their wooden Adirondack chairs which George had painted canary yellow and Velma had made colorful seat cushions. She had picked colors that depicted the colorful view; greens, those of the many evergreen trees that dotted their acreage - along with yellow and orange shades of the magnificent sunsets. They would quietly sit there and watch as the waves moved in and out along the shoreline - so beautiful and picturesque that many an artist has captured the essence of it on canvas.

The waves of the Pacific Ocean would change when high winds were present. They would crash with great fury against the huge rock formations that jut out of the floor of the Pacific and are positioned along the shoreline. That familiar sound could be heard from their front porch. The white-capped waves which created an entirely different landscape, but they were just as magnificent.

George would go for a quick swim in the ocean whenever his sinuses gave him fits. He did not understand the medicinal reasons, but the salt water was a definite healing agent for him. He would return home with less symptoms and actually breathing normally.

To the shock of family and community, eight years after George's retirement he was killed in a car accident in downtown Middleton when a large delivery truck ran a red light and 'T-boned' his car on the driver's side. He would live only two days after the accident, leaving Velma a widow in her late sixties. Velma called his death a promotion into Heaven and she planned to meet him there one day. She was not left entirely alone, though, as she still had three of her six married children living in the area.

She once said to her oldest daughter, Cassie, who bemoaned the fact that her mother lived alone, "Cassie, I may feel lonely at times, but I'm never alone when I have the Lord in my heart."

Stephen, the oldest, is a middle-school teacher in Middleton. Another son, Gordon, works at the manufacturing plant where his dad had worked. Sonja, the youngest daughter, is a stay-at-home mom who homeschooled her children and now her grandchildren, but also spends days and hours volunteering with different organizations in Middleton. "She's the spittin' image of her mother," friends would say.

The oldest daughter, Cassie, lives in Seattle with her family and works as a co-host for a morning television talk-show. The second son, Paul, left a career with the Army as a military policeman to join the staff at the Washington State Penitentiary in Walla Walla working his way up to his present position.

Number four son and the youngest child, James, moved to Portland, Oregon after his graduation from college and law school to build a law practice. Life in those larger cities had more to offer the young ones than in the small towns along the Washington coastline.

Since George's death Stephen, the oldest son, and Sonja, the youngest daughter regularly checked on their mother. Gordon had become the handy-man who his mom would call upon whenever she needed something fixed at the house.

She has eighteen grandchildren, eight who still live close by. They love their grandmother, with some of them finding all kinds of reasons to visit her, while others were too involved in their own lives to pay attention to an aging grandmothr. Only when problems arose did those same individuals find time to call her to request prayer. They all thought of her as *one who had a direct line to God.*

Velma only had two siblings still alive - a sister who lives in San Antonio, Texas and a brother who is in a nursing home there in Middleton. She visits her brother at least once a week. She hadn't seen her sister in about three years.

Her life was good, but she felt lonely at times during those first couple of years after George's death. She knew, though, that she was blessed to be a part of a church family who had a great deal of love for one another and a strong faith in God. They encouraged her vision for the future which she knew was in God's hands. When bad days popped up, she would recall the many blessings of the past, which helped her to know that God's love was the same yesterday, today and will be tomorrow. That's not to say that she did not have times when the tears flowed and she would find herself missing George until her heart ached.

The family home seemed very large now that she was alone. But, she could not bring herself to move from the serenity she continued to experience there on the shore of that huge expanse of the Pacific Ocean. The extra bedrooms were perfect for the children and grandchildren who came from out-of-town to spend weekends with her. They had enjoyed the beaches growing up and the sand never did get out of their shoes, so they would still return each year to pick up where they left off as teenagers.

During the summer months, two or more of the out-of-town Pearce children and their families would meet at Pacific Beach, a short distance north of Middleton. They would bringing their tents or RVs to camp out. Pacific Beach, Washington is a small beach community of fewer than a thousand people. Yearly, thousands of tourists enjoy Pacific Beach State Park, a ten-acre camping park with twenty-three hundred feet of ocean shoreline. The daily high temperature in that area during the summer is in the seventies, just right for camping.

Velma could never envision herself living anywhere else but Middleton, as it was so beautiful and held so many warm memories. The town had everything she needed to carry on a normal life in her senior years – Safeway plus two other large supermarkets, WalMart, a mall, McDonalds and many other fast-food restaurants, a couple of dollar stores – that Velma still calls a five-and-dime store, a throwback to her earlier years. There are several drug stores, many nice restaurants, and a good bus service that stops near her home. She has her children and grandchildren living close by, a good Bible-based church to attend, a long-time friend and good doctor, a first-rate hospital *and* an abundance of friends - what more could she want?

Chapter 3

Velma lay on her back on the ER examination table as a doctor and two nurses worked on her. Her body was limp, her eyes closed and her breathing shallow. One of the nurses connected her to an IV drip and within minutes a lab technician had retrieved a couple of vials of her blood.

The nurse cleaned the mud from Velma's face which revealed abrasions on her forehead and right cheek. After cleansing the mud from her nose and the blood from under her nose, she thought *I think this lady's nose may be broken.* She backed away from the bed as the doctor entered the cubicle and she spoke to him about the nose.

The physician asked, "Has she come to, at all?"

"No."

"I want a CAT-scan of her head 'stat' to check for any swelling, internal hemorrhaging or maybe an aneurism."

Making a note of that, she replied, "Yes, sir. Will she also need an MRI?"

"Possibly." He bent over Velma and in a slow, but distinct voice said, "Mrs. Pearce, can you hear me?"

There was no reaction from Velma.

"Do you know where you are?"

There was still no response. Again, "Mrs. Pearce, Can you hear me?" He shook his head and let out a big sigh.

The doctor then examined her nose with a special instrument for that purpose. Then as he touched her nose he heard a crackling sound like that of rubbing hair between two fingers. That was significant and together with the small of amount of blood the nurse had wiped away from the patient's nostrils to confirm his suspicions of a fractured nose. As he looked closer, he detected a slight swelling taking place. He wrote an order on her chart for an ice pack to be applied to that area.

He clicked his pen closed, placed it in his jacket pocket and returned the clipboard to its slot at the end of the bed. He left the cubicle with directions to get her to x-ray, immediately.

Within minutes after Velma's return to the cubicle from x-ray, Stephen, her eldest son pulled back the curtain and went to her bedside. With one look at his mother, he gasped. He could barely stomach the sight of her in that condition.

Stephen leaned over and kissed his mother's forehead and then whispered, "Mother? It's Stephen." He waited, but she did not reply. "Mother, open your eyes, please. It's me, Stephen."

In exasperation, he turned toward the nurse, "Is she going to be okay?"

The nurse just shook her head. "I'm sorry, but we don't have the results of all the tests, as yet."

Stephen pulled a chair up close to the bed and had no sooner sat down than the doctor returned. He nodded his head in recognition of Stephen and then walked to Velma's bedside. "Are you Mrs. Pearce's son?"

"Yes, sir, I'm Stephen Pearce," standing and offering his hand.

"Mr. Pearce, I'm Dr. Swanson."

"How is she, doctor?"

"Right now she is still unconscious, so we can't ascertain from her where she might be hurting in places other than what we've detected. Excuse me just a minute. I need to get her ankle taped up. She has a slight fracture of the right ankle. She also has a broken nose."

Stephen sat there holding his mother's hand, anxious to know the prognosis for his mother's recovery. At the same time he took notice and admired the teamwork of the doctor and nurse as they worked together on his mother. Part way through the procedure, the doctor looked over at Stephen to catch his eye and then nodded his head in the direction of the entrance to the cubicle. Stephen understood and followed him out.

"Doctor, what happened to my mother?"

"From what the emergency technician told me, she was knocked down by a little boy on his bicycle. It appears to be an accident. From the results of tests we now know more about her injuries and it looks as though her right side hit the ground first. Her right shoulder is dislocated and quite bruised. Her right hip is broken and so is her right ankle.

"The ambulance attendant told me that her head landed in the mud while the rest of her body was on the sidewalk. She was lucky that she wore a heavy coat that day, as it protected her from being scraped-up any more than she is."

That word *lucky* sent a shiver through Stephen. His position as a teacher kicked in and he wanted to correct the speaker. *Lucky* was not a word allowed by members of the Pearce family. 'Christians aren't lucky, they are blessed,' his mother would admonish whenever she heard a family member use that *word*. He jerked his attention back to the conversation at-hand.

"Mr. Pearce, your mother is still unconscious and we can only believe she'll be lucky enough . . . "

Before the doctor could finish his sentence, Stephen interrupted him with a hand held up to indicate - stop.

"Forgive me, sir, but if my mother heard you say she was *lucky* one more time, you might be in deep trouble. She's a Christian and she would straight out say to you, 'I am not lucky. I am blessed.'"

The doctor looked down at his shoes, holding his gaze there for a moment and then looked back up at Stephen. He nodded his head; his lips tightened and then he said, "You're right. I guess *we* have a bad habit of using that word. I'm a Christian, too, but I've never had anyone to bring me up short about it. Thank you."

Stephen felt a pang of guilt to have spoken up as he did. "I apologize, sir. I didn't mean to be rude."

"No. No. You were right to correct me," the doctor said as he placed his right hand on Stephen's shoulder. "I appreciate you being forthright with me."

Stephen smiled.

"Getting back to your mother's head injury, she has a concussion with some swelling of the brain, which I hope doesn't proceed any further. So we'll wait for a day or so to do the surgery on her hip. As for the shoulder, I'm waiting for the orthopedic surgeon to further evaluate the tests. She'll be in ICU until she comes to, then we'll put her into her own room."

"Doctor, I'd like my mother to have a private room, if possible. She has so many family members who will want to visit with her and I wouldn't want that to disturb another patient in the room."

"That can be arranged. I need to attend to another patient right now, but I'll be back to see your mother in a few minutes."

Stephen sat down in the chair and could only stare at his mother. *She looks so fragile.* His attention was then drawn to a hand pulling back the curtain. An attendant pushed a gurney to Velma's bedside. "We've come to take Mrs. Pearce to ICU." He lifted her arm to check the medical band on her wrist to make sure he had the right patient.

Stephen rose from the chair and stepped back out of the way, as the attendant and a nurse began a slow, methodical pace to slide Velma's frail body onto the gurney. Stephen winced as they moved her, not wanting any further pain inflicted upon his beloved mother.

The gurney was wheeled along the aisle toward the elevator, with Stephen following behind. Before they reached it, Sonja, the youngest Pearce daughter, flew toward them. Entering the main door, she had caught sight of her brother and knew that the person on the gurney had to be her mother.

"Mama. Are you okay?" asked Sonja.

Stephen spoke up, "Sonja, she's unconscious."

Sonja covered her mouth with her hand, startled at her mother's appearance. Then, "Stephen," she blurted out, "She doesn't even look like Mama."

"Calm down, Sonja. Her face is swollen from a broken nose."

Stephen lifted his hand motioning Sonja to move back so that the attendant could continue on to the elevator." Stephen began, again, "They're taking her to ICU."

"Oh. Okay," she replied as she walked alongside the gurney.

Waiting for the elevator, Sonja leaned down and kissed her mother's forehead. "Rick and Cheri will be coming to see you as soon as they get off work." She could only hope that her mother heard her.

Two attendants got Velma settled into her new surroundings, and had just left when Dr. Jordan, Velma's family doctor of twenty-five years, knocked on the doorjamb and entered the room. He was semi-retired at the present time.

"Stephen. Sonja. It's so good to see you, but not under these circumstances. The hospital called me to inform me that I had a patient here."

"I told them that you were mother's primary physician."

Turning his attention to Velma, Dr. Jordan said, "What happened?"

Stephen related the scenario he had received from Dr. Swanson and also the facts of her injuries.

"Hmm. Sounds like she'll be here a while." He turned back to Velma, his forehead furrowed by a deep frown of concern for what he was observing.

"I only wish she would've let me drive her to the grocery store, and then this wouldn't have happened," sighed Sonja.

"Ah, come on, Sis. No need to do the could've, would've, should've game."

"I know."

Chapter 4

Cassie Graham, Velma's oldest daughter, and Bill Hudson were on the set at the television station in downtown Seattle where the two co-anchor a morning talk-show. Cassie stepped down from the set as the program went to a commercial. Bill, by himself, would have the next three-minute segment by himself interviewing the superintendent of schools.

Even at age sixty, her beauty radiated, from her warm smile to her stunning creamy complexion. Today, every lovely strand of Cassie's auburn hair was in place and she dressed in a soft shade of periwinkle, which accented her hair - she looked like a runway model.

Her degree in communications had landed her a job with a radio station at first, but when a spot opened up at a television station, owned by the same company, she applied and got the job. She was a hit with the audience right from the start with her infectious laugh and her captivating way with words.

Cassie seemed to be made for television. She did not strut with pride over her accomplishments, but seemed to appreciate all that life had presented her.

She and her co-anchor, Bill, had worked together for the past two years and a great charisma existed between them which seemed to make the individuals they interviewed very much at ease.

Cassie reached for the cup of lukewarm coffee which she had left earlier on a table just out of camera view. After a sip, she took a big deep breath as her thoughts went to the next segment of the program. And then, just as Bill was wrapping up his interview, a production assistant handed Cassie a note.

At first, she started to tuck it in her jacket pocket to save until the next commercial break, but instead opened the folded piece of paper and began to read. She walked toward her chair on the set, careful to step over the maze of electrical cables that run from the cameras and zigzagged their way across the studio floor. Then she stopped - dead still in her tracks - her mouth gaped open. She could hardly breathe.

"Bill, you'll have to go on without me."

"What! What'ta ya mean?"

Waving the note in the air and darting off in the other direction, she yelled back, "I need to leave. I just heard that my mother is in a coma in the hospital."

"Sure, kid, go. I hope everything turns out all right."

"Thanks."

"Cassie?"

She turned back toward Bill.

"Think I need to go solo again tomorrow?"

"Probably. I'll give you a call later."

"Sure. You get goin'. Drive carefully." Cassie pulled her cell phone from her jacket pocket and speed dialed her husband's cell phone number. She impatiently waited for him to answer.

"Bob. Bob, I gotta go to Middleton. My mother's had an accident and is in the hospital. I'm going to run by the house and get a couple of changes of clothes and then head out."

"Tell ya what, I'll meet you down there in the morning. I'll finish up here tonight so that I can stay down there for another day or so, if need be."

"Oh, great. Thanks, sweetheart. I'll need you there." She walked down the hallway toward her boss's office as she continued her conversation.

"Who called and told you about your mother?"

"Marianne.

"Was it a car accident?"

"No. She said that a little boy on his bike hit Mama and knocked her down to the ground. She's unconscious, Bob."

"Well, honey, sometimes being unconscious is the best thing if there's head trauma. It gives the brain time to heal. You'd better get going. I'll see you sometime tomorrow morning. Please, Cassie, drive carefully."

"You know I'm a good driver."

"Yes, you are. But right now you're in an emotional state and that means you need to pay closer attention to your driving and not let your mind wander."

"I hear you. Love you. Bye."

"Love you, too."

Cassie touched the 'off' button and slid her phone back into her jacket pocket. She rushed into her boss's office to tell him of her plight.

The traffic on Interstate Highway 5, heading south out of Seattle, was bumper-to-bumper, but after passing Sea-Tac International Airport it began to thin out. Cassie was then able to relax her hands on the steering wheel and lower her shoulders back against the seat. As she continued on toward Tacoma her mind began to drift off to thoughts of despair at the possibility of her mother dying.

"Stop it," she said aloud. "Whew. Cassie, you can't go there. I need to be praying instead." Her eyes darted upward for a second. "Sorry, Lord." She clenched her lips together tightly, took a deep breath and did her best to calm down so that she could pray.

She had learned over her many years of experience in serving the Lord that praying for His will was the only way to go, so that's how she started. "Father, you know how much I love my mother and want everything to be okay, but I'm also aware that You love her even more. But, my heart's desire is for Your will to be done. If you're not through with Mama yet, I ask that Your healing hand be extended to her. I . . ."

She was cut off from praying when a car cut in front of her much too close for comfort. *Stupid driver! Oops, sorry, Lord.* She did not continue to pray after that close encounter, but reached over and pushed the 'on' button for the CD player. She listened to her favorite music from The Brooklyn Tabernacle Choir. Her body relaxed again as those beautiful blended voices brought a heavenly calm to her spirit and emotions.

Just outside Olympia, she pulled into a drive-thru restaurant to get a sandwich. She was hungry, as she always ate breakfast very early in order to be at the television station by six. She also ordered a large coffee, knowing that she needed to stay alert on the next stretch of the highway, especially now that rain was falling. She pulled into one of the restaurant's parking spaces to relax for a few minutes while she ate her lunch.

She no sooner got back on the highway when her cell phone rang. She picked it up from the passenger seat and answered it. Concentrating on the road, she didn't look to see who was calling. "Cassie speaking."

"Hey, sweetheart, it's me."

"Hold on, Bob. I need to pull over to the shoulder of the road." On a number of occasions, Cassie had interviewed parents of teens killed in car accidents caused by either talking or texting on a cell phone while driving. Her thoughts would always go to her own children and she could not imagine how devastating that would be for her if she was to lose a child to death. Those vivid reports had left her with an indelible mark on her mind and a resolve to never allow cell phones to distract her while driving.

Bob had called to just say 'hi' and to make sure that she was okay. They talked for just a couple of minutes and then Cassie got back on the road. She would soon need to turn right off Interstate Highway 5 onto Highway 8, which would take her to Highway 12, and then on to Middleton.

As Cassie drew closer to her hometown, the rain ceased and she began to smile at the familiar sights and especially the smells. She lowered the driver's-side window and drank in the familiar smell of the ocean. *Ahh, the ocean.*

That smell immediately brought back a memory of the last time that she and her dad were together on a father-daughter outing – just prior to her wedding, many years earlier.

That day had started out with fog hovering over the area – nothing unusual about that. The two finished breakfast and then secured buckets, rakes and small shovels from the shed behind the house. The sun had begun to penetrate the dense blanket of fog by that time.

They climbed down the cliff, George checking back every few steps to make sure that Cassie was making the descent okay. By the time they reached the sandy beach, the fog had dissipated and as they looked out at the ocean, the sun was reflecting off the water and it appeared as though millions of sparkling diamonds danced on the rippling waves.

As that memory continued, Cassie smiled as she recalled *Daddy asked question after question that day about my impressions of what the future held for Bob and me.* Aloud she said, "Oh, Daddy. I miss you so."

The memory of that special day with her dad was like a shot of adrenaline; rejuvenating her and eliminating the heaviness that had engulfed her since she received that earlier call from Marianne. *Middleton and the ocean are still a big part of my being.* She smiled.

It was mid-afternoon when Cassie pulled into the hospital parking lot and her expression changed to one of worry. She thought *I'm not sure I want to go in there and see Mama in such bad condition.* Her friends and family knew her to be a tower of strength, just like her dad. At this moment, though, she felt more weak-kneed than she had ever experienced before. She didn't like that feeling.

Then, she nodded as she remembered something her dad had once said to her when she was disheartened over losing to someone else in a spelling bee. "Cassie, your life in Middleton, with all of its ups and downs, has prepared you for whatever life will place in front of you."

He was right she thought. She smiled, switched off the ignition, grabbed her purse from the seat beside her and took a deep breath - letting it out slowly. She then got out and headed for the hospital's front door walking around puddles of water left by the earlier rain.

The receptionist looked up Velma Pearce's name in the registry and told Cassie that her mother was in ICU on the second floor.

The hospital staff had changed shifts a half-hour earlier and when Cassie approached the nurse's station, everyone was still busy viewing patient's charts to prepare for their rounds. Cassie stood there for a couple of moments before anyone noticed her.

"I'm sorry. May I help you?"

"Yes, ma'am. I'm Cassie Graham, Mrs. Pearce's daughter. Where is she?"

"Oh, yes, Mrs. Graham. Your brother has been expecting you," she said as she pointed out to her the double doors right beside the nurse's station.

Chapter 5

Across town in a small two-bedroom apartment, heaviness filled the air in the bedroom of Tony Ramirez. He sat on his bed cross-legged, his head bent and eyes staring at the Washington Husky football-team logo in the middle of his quilt. *If she dies, I'll go to prison and who will be here to help my mom?* At thirteen, boys are told not to cry, but on that fateful day he could not hold back the tears running down his cheeks. He was alone; his mother was at work until seven that evening.

Earlier in the day when the ambulance had left with Mrs. Pearce, the police had driven him home. His mother, who worked at a convenience store on the outskirts of town, was home getting ready to go to work on the eleven-to-seven shift when a knock came at her door.

Who could that be? With her hairbrush still in her hand, she opened the front door and was taken aback by the sight of two policemen standing there with her son in between them.

"Mrs. Ramirez?"

"Yes. What is it, officer?" she said, in her very distinct Spanish accent. Then she looked at Tony and said, "What've you done? Why aren't you in school?"

"May we come in?"

"Um . . . ah, yes, please come in."

"Mrs. Ramirez, we need to talk to you about an accident your son had a little while ago."

Consuela sat down in the armchair, her hand over her mouth. She turned to look at Tony, "Are you all right?"

"Yes, Mama. I'm okay."

She turned back to the police. "What kind of accident?"

"He was riding his bike and his handlebar hit an elderly lady and she's in the hospital. It was an accident, ma'am, as far as we know. Your son said he did not realize he was that close to her as he rode by."

Her head swiveled back and forth from the policeman giving the explanation of the accident to her one and only son, who was sitting dejectedly on the sofa. At times she was not even hearing what was being said.

"Is the lady going to be all right?"

"We don't know, ma'am. Right now, we do have some paperwork that needs to be filled out."

"Paperwork?"

"Yes, ma'am. A report needs to be submitted to the police department for investigation of the accident."

"I'm sorry, but I should be on my way to work. Please excuse me a moment while I call to tell them I'll be late."

Sergeant Jackson, a seasoned cop with many years of experience, sat down on the sofa beside Tony and put his large hand on Tony's back, patting him gently. "It was an accident, son. It could have happened to anyone. You mustn't blame yourself." He could only assume that it was an accident, until further examination of the evidence.

It was comforting to Tony to have a man, at this moment in time, to be a father-figure who understood him and to even call him 'son'. His dad had left him and his mother several years earlier, and he always yearned to have a father.

Tony did not look up, but fixed his eyes on the carpet below his feet.

The taller of the policemen, a rookie said, "Sarge, I'll go out and get Tony's bike out of the trunk." Looking at Tony, he asked, "Where should I put it?"

Tony lifted his eyes slightly and said, "In my bedroom. That's where I keep it."

"All right."

Mrs. Ramirez put down the phone receiver and returned to her chair.

"My partner went out to the car to get Tony's bike."

She nodded her head in understanding. Turning to Tony, she asked, "Why weren't you in school?"

Still looking down at the floor he mumbled, "I didn't have my science project finished and I didn't want the teacher to know it, so I skipped school after second period."

Mrs. Ramirez closed her eyes and shook her head in disbelief. "You told me last night that the project was finished."

"I know. But it wasn't."

"You've lied, skipped school, and you've hurt someone. What else have you done? What other bad news am I going to hear?"

"I'm sorry, Mama."

"'Sorry' won't help you, this time."

The front door opened and the rookie carried in the bike. "Which way to your room, Tony?"

Tony got up to escort him down the hallway. As he passed by the front door, he really wanted to bolt out of the apartment, but knew that he was already in deep trouble.

The sergeant began filling out the necessary paperwork. "Mrs. Ramirez, what's your husband's first name?"

"You won't need that information. He's been long gone from us and I have no idea where he is."

"Are you divorced?"

"No, sir. But, might as well be. I've raised Anthony on my own since he was a little boy. I'm assuming the bum went back to Mexico."

"Anthony? Is Tony a nickname?"

"Yes."

"Your full name, please."

"Consuela Ramirez."

"Are you a U.S. citizen?"

"I am," she replied emphatically. "I studied hard and passed the test about five years ago. I knew that I needed to stay in this country to give my son a good education. Worked hard every moment I could at the library studying for the test. I'm very proud to be a U. S. citizen," she said with a smile.

"That's wonderful, Mrs. Ramirez. But, I'll still need your husband's name."

"Jose Rodriguez Ramirez."

"You say you don't have any idea where he is right now?"

"That's right."

When all the questions were answered and signatures affixed to the paperwork, Sergeant Jackson stood up. "Tony, if that lady decides to press charges against you, you'll be receiving a summons to appear in juvenile court." Turning to Mrs. Ramirez, he continued. "Please, make sure he gets there."

"Oh, I will."

The men made their way to the front door. Sgt. Jackson turned to Tony, placing his hand on his shoulder, "Don't miss any more school. Your mother has worked hard to give you a good education, so don't let her down. It's better that you take the punishment given out for a late project than to bring disappointment to your mother. Do you understand me?"

Tony nodded his head rapidly. "Yes, sir. What's going to happen to me?"

"Don't know, son."

All Tony could do was to heave a big sigh of despair.

Back inside the apartment behind closed doors, mother and son sat down at the kitchen table. "Tony, what am I going to do with you? This is the second time you've gotten yourself into trouble, but thankfully the first time the police were not involved. This time you may have to go to court. What if you get sent to reform school? You aren't going to like that one bit."

Tony sat silent, not even looking at his mom. He knew that nothing he said would help the situation.

"The rent is due next week, so I've got to get to work. I'll be home at the regular time and I expect to see your science project - finished."

"Yes, ma'am."

She started for the door and then turned. "I love you, Tony and I really do care about what happens to you."

"Love you, too, Mom."

"That blue dish in the refrigerator has some left-over stew in it. Just put a smaller bowl of it in the microwave for your supper. I'll call you on my break."

"Okay."

Tony was glad she was gone. But, now the deathly silence in the apartment only gave way to the many horrible thoughts that ran through his mind. *What if I killed that lady? What will the judge do to me?*

It would be a long, lonely afternoon and evening for Tony. He had promised his mother to finish the science project, so he pulled the box holding all the items from under his bed. *Guess I'll set it up on the kitchen table.*

Chapter 6

It was a few minutes after eleven that morning when James Pearce, Velma's youngest, received the alarming news about his mother. He had just left the courtroom during a break in the session and had gone out into the hall to make a call to a witness who had not shown up for a trial. He finished the call and pushed the 'off' button. Before he could put the phone in his inside jacket pocket, a call had come through. He didn't recognize the number, but decided to answer it anyway.

"James Pearce."

"James, this is Marianne."

"Hey, Marianne, I didn't recognize the phone number. What's up?"

"James, your mother was in an accident and she's in the hospital."

"How bad is she hurt?"

"They aren't sure as yet."

"Who's there with her?"

"Stephen. I think Sonja will be there in just a few minutes."

"Oh, dear. I'm in the midst of a trial." Speaking to Marianne, but more out loud to himself, he said, "I'll need to get with my associate to replace me for today and tomorrow. A friend of mine has a plane, so I'll ask him to fly me up there. That'll be quicker than trying to get a commercial flight out of Portland."

"Okay. Stephen will keep you informed about your mother as soon as he knows more."

"Great."

Marianne conveyed to him what she knew of the accident and then they said their goodbyes.

James has an impressive reputation in Portland, having won so many high-profile cases as a defense lawyer. Women especially love to have him as their lawyer, as he is tall, handsome and dark-haired, with a little greying around the temples. He has always relished his prestigious standing in the community and carried himself in a proud manner. Because of that, some people, especially men, were put off by his seemingly arrogant ways. He was characterized by some as being inclined to emphasize faults, raise objections and insist proof be shown to him – which of course is his job, but was always carried to excess. He was a real pain in the side of the local court system.

He and his wife, Wanda, live in a large mansion in the up-scale section of Portland, a location which is very important to James. They have two children; each has acquired a successful career after college. It seems to James and Wanda that life is like a hot-fudge sundae with whipped cream and a cherry on top - a real delicious life.

They both loved to be seen at charity and civic events or at restaurants frequented by those who are 'in the know'. One of their favorite places to dine out is at the Nostrana, owned and operated by Cathy Whims, who is a highly-acclaimed chef in the Northwest.

After receiving Marianne's call, James called his law partner first, then his wife and lastly his friend who owned a plane. Those calls completed, he went back to his office where he always kept a spare razor, after-shave and a set of clothes for when he would have to make a quick trip out of town for legal purposes. He packed them away in a small suitcase and headed for the airport.

Velma loves her youngest child, but only sees him on occasions. He is consistent about calling her each Sunday afternoon, but she would prefer a visit from him.

When George was still alive, he once said, "James and Wanda may be living the high life, but without their acknowledgement of the Lord in their lives, their balloon will burst one of these days.

"He seems to be walking around in a spiritual fog, not able to discern his own need of a Heavenly Father. I'm surprised and disappointed. I had such high hopes that the exuberance he exhibited during his teens as the leader of the youth group at church would continue in college. But, not so."

Velma's reply was, "I know. I only hope he comes back to the Lord, like the Prodigal Son did in the Bible, before it's too late. We can only pray and trust God to take care of that matter."

Paul Pearce, Velma's second son, received the call regarding his mother at his office at the prison just after he had finished questioning a prisoner regarding an incident in a cell block.

"Paul Pearce. How may I help you?"

"Paul, this Marianne."

"Hey, girl. How are you?"

"I'm fine, but your mother isn't. She's had an accident and is in the hospital. Stephen is with her and he asked me to call all of you to let you know."

"How is Mother?"

"Too soon to tell. She's in a coma and they are running tests."

"Marianne, let Stephen know that I'm on my way. I'll stop by and pick up Sandy and we should be there in a couple of hours."

"Okay. Stephen said he would text you from time to time as to her condition."

"That'll be great. In the meantime, we need to send up a lot of prayers for Mom. She prayed long and hard for the six of us while we were growing up and only God knows how we would have turned out if she hadn't. She taught us well, Marianne.

"How did it happen?"

Marianne shared the details that Stephen had related to her and then they ended the call.

Paul put down the receiver, only to pick it up again to call the warden to let him know he needed to leave. Then he called Sandy to have her pack a few things for the trip to Middleton. "Sandy, text the kids about Mom's accident." Two of their children lived in the area and one in New York.

Gordon Pearce, Velma's third son, had received his call from Marianne, and as supervisor, he handed down the reins to the next in command and headed out to the parking lot. Before driving to the hospital he called his wife, Trisha, to head over there as well.

Gordon was labeled by his siblings as a home-body. He loved going home at night after work to spend time with his family when they were growing up. His two boys and daughter were the delight of his life. The boys played in little league baseball, took wrestling when in high school, while the daughter spent her time outside of regular classes in choir and in many of the school plays. After graduation, one son and his daughter went on to college, while the youngest joined the Navy. Gordon used to say about his youngest, "I guess living so close to the Pacific Ocean, he got seawater in his veins and wanted to sail the seven seas."

Velma could count on Gordon to fix anything and everything that would go wrong with her house after George died. He took after his dad in that respect. She loved his sense of humor, which raised her spirits each time they were together. Even growing up, his lively attitude brought laughter into any family gathering. He got that from his mom.

Gordon's 1988 Dodge Ram 318 pickup purred right along as it sailed through traffic on the way into town. *This bucket of bolts has given me good service. Didn't think she'd last this long. Needs a coat of paint, but other than that, she's been a real winner.* He smiled.

Gordon's thoughts then drifted off to his Mom and Christmas, as it was just a few weeks away. She always made it the event of the year. Even after her kids had kids of their own, she would do special things with the little ones. She would invite only them to spend a December Saturday with her to help bake Christmas goodies. She had enough cookie cutters so that each child could cut out a particular shape in the cookie dough. Stars, Santas,

Christmas trees and gingerbread men pressed into that dough brought squeals of delight from the younger ones and smiles of gratification from the older ones. They watched the egg timer tick, tick, tick away. They wanted to see the final stage of their endeavors, but the truth of the matter was - they really wanted to sample them.

It began to rain as Gordon reached the city limits. He smiled as he drove, recognizing how blessed he was to have been brought up in a home full of love. He had carried on some of those same familiar Christmas traditions with his own family. His wife, Trisha, came from a large, but poor family and had never experienced the kind of family celebrations that he did. She allowed her husband to lead the way in their holiday festivities. She loved the reactions from the children when trimming the tree together and the reading of the Christmas story from the Bible before they went to bed on Christmas Eve. It made her feel like a kid. *Can't believe that Christmas is only two months away* he thought.

He pulled up and stopped for a red light at the busiest intersection of Middleton. The light changed to green, but he was still too absorbed in his thoughts to be aware that it had. The driver in the car behind him finally honked their horn. Gordon looked up and saw the green light, then he looked in the mirror and waved his right hand to signify - *sorry, I'm on my way.*

Gordon stepped on the gas and immediately the pickup began to spit and sputter. "Hey, what's goin' on here?" He pushed harder on the gas pedal, hoping that giving it a little more gas would bring it out of this awkward situation. But, not so. The engine died and it was very difficult to steer the pickup. He stepped on the brake, which did not take hold as when the engine was running. He was able to bring the vehicle to a stop – right in the middle of that busy intersection. *This is awful.* Horns began honking only making Gordon feel even worse.

Whoa! This is so embarrassing. He got out of the truck to push it over to the side of the road, when he noticed two men in the car behind him also get out. *Oops! Hope they're in a good mood.*

They surprised Gordon when in the midst of the pouring rain, one man began to stop traffic in the right-hand lane, while the other man, dressed in business attire, helped Gordon push the pickup over to the curb. The driver returned to his car and pulled it over in front of the disabled truck. Gordon walked up to the passenger's window to say 'thanks' and the passenger lowered his window. The driver, with a nod of his head in the direction of the backseat, yelled over to Gordon, "Get in." The three men were soaked.

"Thanks, fellas. You were lifesavers. Sorry that you got so wet," said Gordon, shaking hands with each one.

The driver said, "You know, I almost ran into you when your vehicle died, but luckily I was hardly moving at that point. Hey, don't I know you?" He paused. "You look so familiar"

Gordon took a good look at the Good Samaritan, "You look familiar, too. I'm Gordon Pearce."

"Aha. You're George and Velma's son, right?"

Gordon nodded. "Yes, sir."

"I'm Cal Phillips. I was the lawyer at the probate court for the reading of your dad's will. I remember seeing you there."

"You've got a good memory."

"It's been said that I do." He turned to the other man, "This is my paralegal, Samuel Duncan. We just came from court. Say, what happened to your truck?"

"Not sure. I need to check it out."

"Go ahead and we'll wait to see if you need any help."

Gordon got back into the driver's seat of his pickup and tried to start it. Nothing. His eyes drifted down to the gas gauge and was shocked. *Oh, no - I'm out of gas.* He shook his head in disbelief. *I was gonna get gas at lunch today.* He had planned to use his lunch-hour that day to pick up some new hardware for his mom's kitchen cabinets and – get some gas. The previous week had been an unusually busy one where he had used the pickup more often than just going to and from work. He had told his wife on many occasions, "I *never* let the gas tank get below a quarter of a tank." *If she were here right now she'd probably say,* "Darling, this is one of those 'never' say 'never' moments - right?"

With a sheepish grin he got back out of his vehicle and back into the lawyer's car, where he shared his embarrassing news with the two gentlemen.

"Been there and done that," said the legal assistant. "Of course, it was when I had a girl out on a date."

"Ah, go on," said the lawyer. "You just made that up."

"Yup."

All three had to chuckle over that old fabricated 'male-tale'.

"Can I drive you to get some gas?"

"That would be much appreciated. I was on my way to the hospital. My mother was in an accident just a little while ago."

"Then we need to hurry."

Gordon shared what little he knew about his mother's accident with the two men as they made their way to the nearest service station. He had grabbed a jerry can out of the back of his pickup and now filled it with gas.

On the way back, Gordon took that time to call his brother, Stephen. Then he sat back and stared out the side window.

His thoughts were interrupted by the lawyer. "Gordon, I just remembered something about your mother. She's in that guardian ad litem program, right?"

"Yes."

"I've heard some good things about her caring ways with those kids."

"She takes her job seriously. Right after my dad died, she needed something to do that would set her mind on to someone else, instead of herself."

"Some of those kids are in trouble with the law, while others are bound by a troubled home," the lawyer explained.

"She loves what she does. She came from a big family of children, raised six kids herself, and when Dad passed away her attention was drawn to the CASA organization. She told me that she had actually talked with my Dad on different occasions about wanting to help them out in some tangible way. Now she's put those desires to work."

"Wished more people would see the need to get involved with our kids today," said the lawyer.

"I know what ya mean. Parents seem to be too busy anymore makin' a livin', 'stead of bein' real parents. They leave parenting up to the schools, and the schools can't be taxed with that responsibility. The kids wind up raising themselves and they surely don't have the wherewithal to make good decisions. Whatever feels good - that's what they do," shared Gordon.

"You're right, there. I've got two pre-teens myself, so I'm aware of such a mindset." He pulled his car up to the curb behind Gordon's truck.

Gordon got out and then spoke to the two men at the driver's window. "Fellas, I think you two need to go and get on some dry clothes. I'm going to get on to the hospital. Thanks again. You've been lifesavers today."

"Gordon, if there's anything I can do for you or your mother, please let me know," said the young lawyer.

"Pray."

With an obvious awkward look on his face, the lawyer said, "Oh . . . ah . . . sure."

Gordon checked his wrist watch as he walked to his pick-up and saw that he had been delayed a little over a half hour getting the gas. As he turned the key in the ignition he realized that he was only five blocks from the hospital. *Maybe I should've left this baby sitting there and walked on to the hospital instead of wasting time getting gas. Just hope Mom is okay. But . . . I guess there's been no change or Stephen would've called or texted me.*

Chapter 7

The ICU critical care nurse came in and observing the five people at Velma's bedside, softly spoke to Stephen, "I'm sorry, but we can only allow two people in here at a time with her. The others can stay in the waiting room down the hall."

Sonja looked at Cassie and said, "I've been with her for a while. You stay here with Stephen. I'll wait my turn."

"Me, too," replied Marianne and Trisha.

The nurse turned back to the trio saying, "Keep talking to her. Recall memories of the past. Sing. Recite her favorite poems. That will keep her mind active, even in her unconscious state."

Sonja, Marianne and Trisha had no sooner left the room than they saw Gordon getting off the elevator. He hurried toward the ladies, giving them each a hug.

He looked at his sister, Sonja. "How is she?"

"The same, Gordon. They'll only allow two people to be in there with her at a time, so we are just heading to the waiting room."

"Who's with her now?"

"Stephen and Cassie. They will come out in a little while and we'll take turns sitting with Mom."

"Okay." He took hold of his wife's hand as they walked down the hallway.

Sitting down among three other individuals in the waiting room, Marianne said, "I talked with Paul and

James, and they should both be here in a little while. James has a friend flying him up here. He was in the middle of a trial, so it may be awhile before he can get everything arranged so that he can leave. Paul was leaving Walla Walla as soon as he picked up Sandy."

For the next twenty minutes or so, the air in the waiting room was filled with anxiety as they sat pondering the future of their injured loved one. They tried to make small-talk, but it was as though no one was really listening that intently to each other. Gordon paced the floor and often left the room to saunter up and down the hall.

Sonja got up and walked to the coffee pot that was placed there for visitors. She picked up the pot and took a whiff of the coffee. "Ooh, this has been sitting here awhile. I'm going down to the cafeteria to get some real coffee. Hey, anyone for coffee? Fresh coffee, that is." She smiled as she put down the coffee pot and looked around the room at not only her own family, but to the other individuals in the room. "I'm taking orders." Only a couple of people took her up on her kind gesture, and she wrote down their orders for coffee with sugar and/or cream.

Sonja is the type of person who has to be busy at all times albeit with constructive works. She rushed, which was her usual pace, to the elevator. She knew exactly where she was headed, as over the years she had visited others in that building from her church family, the kids' school chums or parents, neighbors, and even her own family members. She felt as though she could make her way around the hospital with her eyes closed.

She passed by the door to the chapel on her way to the cafeteria, and a few feet past it she stopped, turned around and decided to go back and go in. She had been moving at a fast pace ever since receiving the phone call about her mother. *Need to spend a couple of minutes with you, Lord,* was how she started her prayer after sitting down and taking a big deep breath. *I know how much You love my mother, but also how much we love her, too. She has been the one who has encouraged me all my life. I couldn't bear the thought of losing her. If you're not through with her here on earth, I'm asking that she be allowed to stay here for a while longer. There are family members and neighborhood friends who still need her loving and gentle admonishment to live a godly life. One last thing, Lord, please help me not to get in a fearful state over my mother's condition. Help my unbelief!* With a huge sigh she closed with *thank you, Lord. Amen.*

Sonja smiled as she arose and felt so much lighter as she headed once again toward the cafeteria.

Paul and Sandy loved traveling in the car together, with little or no distractions to interrupt their conversation. Over the years they had taken many trips by car - the Grand Canyon, Yellowstone National Park and Mt. Rushmore, and loved every mile of the way. They learned so much about each other on those trips, a real intimacy grew as they shared their hearts with each other.

Sandy turned in the seat to look directly at Paul, "Was your relationship with your parents always as good as what I've seen over the years?"

"Nah. There was a time when my teenage rebellion took over and we would go head-to-head over things I was doing. It was funny, though, Dad seemed to leave those particular moments up to Mother. He knew that his over-zealous desire to see me toe-the-line brought about a loud and very animated dialogue. But, Mother, on the other hand, being the peace-maker in the home would just sit there and smile before invading my space, and Dad would let her take the reins. He would twiddle his thumbs wanting so much to jump into our conversation at any moment, but he didn't." Paul grinned at the picture he had just painted for his wife.

"Did she ever get mad?"

"Not very often. When she did, she would usually walk out of the room and stay gone until she had calmed down."

"I should do that. I've always been one to fly off the handle when something rubs me the wrong way - but of course you already know that."

"But, you've mellowed over the years."

"That's because there's generally no one at home now but me to get upset about things. By the time you get home in the evening I've already run the scenario in my mind so many times that I've lost sight of whatever got my dandruff up."

Paul reached over and patted her knee. "I love you just the way you are."

"Thank you, sweetie. That's nice to hear. But, it's still something I need to work on."

Paul just smiled and gave her a wink.

"How about indignant? Did your mom ever get indignant?"

"She sure could. Especially when it came to the mistreatment of kids. Ooh, the hair on the back of her neck would stand up if she heard that someone was intentionally harming one of her six kids or other children, for that matter."

They rode in silence for the next little awhile.

"Paul, did you ever get into trouble with the law?"

"Hey, what brought on that question? You seem to be full of them today."

"Just wondering."

"Yes, your obedient husband had a couple of brushes with the law when I was in the Army. I was pretty rebellious when I first joined, but it actually had started in my senior year in high school.

"Dad and I had differences of opinion on most everything and that caused two males to stand their ground like two confrontational moose - neither of us willing to budge an inch. Finally, the month before graduation my dad said, "Get in the car, Paul."

"'Where we goin'?'

"'Just do as I say for once.'

"We rode in silence into the downtown area, where he stopped in front of the post office. I didn't think much of it, as I thought Mom had given him something to mail.

"'Get out,' came Dad's commanding voice. So I got out and followed him into the post office. He didn't head in the direction of the main post office area, but started for the stairs heading down to the basement level. That's when it hit me."

"What?" asked Sandy. Her curiosity was definitely piqued.

"We were headed to the Army and Navy recruitment center. I stopped on one of the stairs and said, 'Dad, I'm not goin' in the military.'

"He said, 'Yes you are, son. I've given you one too many opportunities to turn from your arrogant ways. Your behavior has caused not only problems with the school's administration, but with the police, and with your mom and me. I won't take one more day of you hurting your mom. Now, march.'

"His voice was so imposing, I automatically obeyed."

"So that's how you came to join the Army."

"Yup. Dad did give me the choice of Navy or Army. I had a feeling Dad wanted me to go into the Navy, so I chose the Army on purpose. My arrogance wouldn't stop until a little later. One good thing, I didn't have to report for duty until after I had graduated."

"Paul, you were so spiteful. I'm so surprised."

"Sandy, you met me after I'd been in the Army for two years and had my ears pinned back a couple of times by my first-sergeant. That's when I simmered down and began to toe-the-line. When I met you at Ft. Bragg, I had finally earned another stripe and knew that if I were to keep it and the pay that went with it - I would have to follow Army regs."

"Regs?"

"Regulations."

"Oh. What all did you do in high school to get your dad so all-fired up?"

"It's very painful to talk about, but since you've asked – well . . . ," he said, with a sad demeanor. "I'll never forget that night."

Sandy sat up in the seat and focused her attention on her husband. Empathetically, she asked, "What happened?" She reached over and gently laid her hand on his arm.

"Well, a couple of my buddies and I had just left a Friday night football game. It was the first time Dad had let me drive his car to anything but the grocery store. I was being so careful. Then it happened . . ." He stopped talking and just looked straight forward as he drove.

"Paul . . . Paul, tell me what happened?" She now had both hands squeezing his arm, expecting him to divulge some dark secret from the past. "Tell me, please!"

"Well . . . ," he paused.

"Yes."

"Well, . . . I . . . ah . . . I ran a stop sign and only a few feet away sat a patrol car behind some large bushes. He got me."

"Oh," she groaned as she sat back in her seat feeling let down by such an insignificant story.

"Gotcha! You thought I was going to reveal something very unscrupulous - some juicy tidbit." He sneered at her and then grinned.

Sandy socked him on the shoulder.

"Ouch."

"You deserve worse," she said, with a big smile.

"How about stopping at that drive-in up ahead and I'll treat you to a cup of coffee?"

"What a big spender!" She grinned and he returned the grin. Still unsatisfied, she coaxed him again. "Come on tell me the truth about your escapades in high school."

"Ah, some things I did are better left untold. I had always thought that those pranks and mischief-making were just kid's stuff until I had kids myself. That's when I felt ashamed. I will share with you this one story – and it's true. When I was ten, I took my sister's pet turtle and flushed it down the toilet. I thought it would flush right on out to sea. Little did I know."

She smiled.

He paused for a moment and then asked, "Do you remember when I drove over to Middleton to see my Dad in the hospital the night before he died?"

Sandy nodded her head.

"That night, as I sat by his bedside holding his hand, and with Mom on the other side of the bed, I asked them both to forgive me for all the bad things I had done that had brought them heartache.

"Mom just looked over at me and smiled. 'You know, son, I figured that someday, after you had kids, you would come to realize that our actions do affect other people.'

"I said, 'I know, Mom, and I'm so sorry. How did you ever put up with six kids?' She just grinned.

"Dad couldn't talk because he had on an oxygen mask; he just squeezed my hand and I knew what he meant."

Paul's thoughts suddenly came back to the present. "Do me a favor, sweetheart. Use my cell phone and call Stephen. I need to know how Mom is doing - right now."

> But I say unto you,
> That every idle word
> that men shall speak,
> they shall give account
> thereof
> in the day of judgment.
> For by thy words
> thou shalt be justified,
> and by thy words thou shalt
> be condemned.
>
> *Matthew 12:36-37 KJV*

Chapter 8

At a small airport on the outskirts of Portland, James' friend, Rocky, taxied his Cessna plane from the hangar out onto the tarmac, all the while receiving instructions from the tower in his headset.

Rocky was the one person who James turned to when he had lost a high-profile court case or when there was trouble at home with Wanda. He would call his drinking buddy to meet at their favorite bar in a small town outside of Portland where no one recognized him. Over the course of several hours the two would continue to drink and settle all the problems of the world.

Wanda objected to James being around Rocky, as he seemed to be an unsavory character. She had said to James on many occasions, "Rocky will definitely put a damper on your good reputation in this town." But, when all was said and done, she knew that with his *selective-hearing problem* he would just shrug off her comments and go right on seeing his buddy.

James felt quite comfortable around Rocky, not having to put on any airs, but could just be himself. Rocky, at times, made his money in unscrupulous ways. But James would tell him, "Whoa, I don't want to know that." What he didn't know he wouldn't ever have to testify to if Rocky was ever caught and put on trial.

Now, as James sat in the cockpit of the Cessna admiring Rocky for the ability to fly anywhere at any time, he thought *I may have to invest in a plane. Sure would be simpler to have my own transportation rather than depend upon commercial airlines. It would certainly take a chunk of change to buy one and Wanda would probably fly off the handle if I told her I wanted one. She would probably complain that it would take money away from those many cruises she takes with her girlfriends. Maybe, just maybe, I could convince her that it would pay for itself over the years and we could go places together at a moment's notice.*

His thoughts were interrupted by Rocky saying, "I've been given the clearance to take off."

With the notion of someday owning his own plane, James paid close attention to Rocky's take-off procedure, even asking questions as the plane taxied down the runway.

As the plane lifted into the air, James said, "Rocky, I can't tell you how much I appreciate you flying me to Middleton. Hope this doesn't keep you from something else that you needed to do."

"Didn't have anything else on the agenda today. Been waitin' to resolve a stalemate on a new contract. Hey, James, on another subject, you never told me about your mom's accident. Was she driving?"

"No. The handlebar on a bicycle side-swiped her, twirled her around and down to the ground."

"That sounds nasty."

"Yes. The last I heard she's still unconscious."

"Makes me shudder to think of it."

"Where does your mom live? I've never heard you talk about her," inquired James.

"Can't rightly say where she is. Haven't been in touch with her in over ten years."

"Sorry, I didn't mean to bring up old wounds."

"Don't worry about it. My mother and my ex-wife are two women that *were* in my life, but thankfully they've now gone by the wayside. Good riddance to 'em."

For a moment, James was silent. He could not quite fully grasp the measure of what his friend had just said. Even though he was often too busy to visit his mother, she was still his mother and he respected her for that. "Um, you don't really mean that, do you?"

"Sure do. I'm single and free to do what I want to do without someone organizing my life to suit them."

"Never heard you talk like that before."

Rocky did not answer, but let out a verbal groan. They flew on in silence for the next little while.

"It's finally quit raining," said Rocky as he switched off the windshield wiper. "We're nearin' the airport, James. Better put on your seatbelt."

"Nah. I'll be all right. You've flown this baby a million times. I trust you to take her down safely," to which his friend shrugged his shoulders. *What ever!*

"Middleton, this is N7-0-3. Over."

"N7-0-3 this is Middleton tower. Go ahead."

"N7-0-3 requests landing instructions. Over."

The man in the tower asked for the type of aircraft, altitude and speed and then finished with, "You have clearance to land on runway 16R. Do you copy?"

"Yes, Middleton, runway 16R. Over."

The tower and Rocky completed the landing instructions, and he was set to take his plane down. "Here we go, James." He lined up with the runway and began the final approach.

James began taking mental notes again, this time on the landing procedure. He watched as his pilot-friend reduced the airspeed and the rate of descent to a slow-enough rate to allow for a gentle touchdown.

Suddenly James felt apprehensive and his heart began to race. He did not fully understand why he was having those emotions, as he had flown before in small planes like this many times without such uneasiness. As a lawyer, he had always prided himself on being able to control his emotions, but not at this moment.

Within a minute or so, Rocky had set the Cessna down on the runway. At that very same moment the right tire blew causing the plane to veer to the right and the tail swung to the left. Rocky immediately pushed on the left rudder pedal and used the left brake to try and help straighten out the plane. It all happened within a few seconds.

Earlier, James had unbuckled his seatbelt to reach back and retrieve a court document from of his briefcase. He then sat back and searched through the document for what he was looking for. But now, as the plane veered to the right and with no shoulder harness to restrain him, James' head flew forward and hit the dashboard with such force that it stunned him for a moment. Even so, he could still hear Rocky's voice which was peppered with expletives like what would come from the mouth of a drunk during a rowdy barroom brawl.

Rocky had been too preoccupied when the tire blew to have thought to place his right arm in front of James to restrain him from being pitched forward. He could only yell out, "Hold on, James. We've blown a tire." The plane came to rest on a grassy area. Rocky just sat there, motionless and speechless.

James, too, sat wordless, recognizing that the accident could have been far more serious.

"You okay, James?"

"Yeah. Sure! Here come the emergency vehicles." As he spoke, he felt a pain shoot through the right side of his face.

James' knees were quite weak when he deplaned. He walked a few feet away from the Cessna and then throwing his head back, he took in a big deep breath of fresh air and let it out. *Thank you, Lord.* He was quite surprised by those words, not having spoken to the Lord in a very long time. He shook his head and thought *where'd that come from?*

He tried to open his mouth to speak to Rocky and when he did pain, worse than he had ever experienced before, shot through the right side of his face.

"James," said Rocky, "need to grab your bag out of the plane. There's a pickup truck over here that'll take us to the hangar. The plane'll be towed over there." Walking over to James, "Hey, fella, you've got blood runnin' down your chin. Looks like it's comin' from inside your mouth."

James reached up and felt the sticky goo and as he brought his hand away to reach for the initialed handkerchief he kept in the front suit-jacket pocket, he thought, *how about that, I'm actually a red-blooded American.* He would have smiled, but that would've hurt.

James dabbed at the wound and each time he winced from the pain. He glanced at his watch as he walked back to the plane. *Here I thought I was going to make better time by not flying commercial. Oh, well. I've gotta call Stephen and let him know I'll be late getting there.* He reached into the plane and grabbed his suitcase and briefcase and walked back toward Rocky.

"There's still blood oozin' down the side of your mouth."

This time James just pressed the handkerchief, oh so gently, against the right side of his mouth, hoping to stop the bleeding.

The driver of the pickup came over to James, having noticed he was holding the side of his face. "Are you injured?"

"Yes. Don't think it's too bad, though."

The driver turned to Rocky. "You've got some paperwork to do. I'll take you over to the hangar and you can fill out the accident report."

Sitting in the hangar office, James reached into his inside jacket pocket and pulled out his cell phone to call Stephen. Before he could flip open the lid, his head began to whirl and he became sick to his stomach. He took a deep breath, hoping to curtail the nausea. It didn't help. "Rocky!" That hurt him to speak. A bit disoriented, he looked around for his friend, but when he moved his head, the room spun like a top. He finally yelled out through his teeth, "Rocky! I need to get to a bathroom. I'm gonna throw up."

Rocky jumped up from his chair and was at James' side in a moment to escort him to the men's room. "Come on, fella."

James wretched until nothing more would come up which hurt his jaw all the more. His legs felt like Jell-O as he raised himself up from the commode. He held onto the wall of the bathroom stall as he opened the door and took a couple of steps toward the outside door, and then he felt his knees buckle. Rocky caught him by the arm and held him up.

"James, we need to get you to a doctor. Sure wished you'd worn that seatbelt, man." The two left the bathroom.

"I'll . . . ah . . . I'll just sit down and wait until you get everything taken care of," said James. The excruciating pain was compounded with the nausea that at times overwhelmed him.

Within a few minutes, Rocky stood up and walked over to James. "A cab has been called. Should be here in a minute or so. We're gettin' you to the hospital - pronto."

"Thanks." He leaned his head back against the wall and remained in that position until the taxi arrived. The pain on the side of his head had now grown a lot stronger.

The ride to the hospital was fairly short, but all the while James hoped he wouldn't throw up again - especially in the taxi.

"Hey, cabbie," said Rocky. "Pull up to the ER door, please."

"Gotcha."

Rocky helped James out of the taxi and in through the automatic door that opened for them. Rocky found a chair for James to rest in. "Stay here, James. I'll get you signed in." This took a few minutes as the required paperwork had to be filled out. Rocky had to fetch James' driver's license and insurance card from his wallet.

A wheelchair was pushed up beside James. A male nurse reached down to put his hand under James' arm pit to help him up. "Here we go, sir."

Inside the ER cubicle a female nurse helped get him up and onto the bed. He rested his head slowly against the pillow.

James reached for the nurse's arm. "I'm gonna throw up. Please get me something."

She opened the door to the bedside table and pulled out a small container just for that purpose. "Here ya go, sir," she said as she placed it into James' hand and propped up his head a smidgeon.

James breathed rapidly, hoping to keep down the bile that kept trying to surface. Then, up it came. He was so embarrassed. Finally, he leaned back against the pillow with the hope that nothing else would come up.

Just then a doctor pulled back the curtain and entered the cubicle and walked to James' bedside. "Hello. I'm Dr. Swanson." He looked down at the information on the clipboard and then looked up and over to James, "You're James Pearce?"

"Yes."

"You wouldn't happen to be related to Velma Pearce, would ya?"

"She's my mother."

"Pearce is usually spelled P-i-e-r-c-e, so when I saw your name spelled with an e-a, I just had to ask. Two Pearces, each with a head injury received on the same day and admitted to the same hospital. That's one for the record books." He made more light conversation as he went to work checking out the injury to James' head. Every time the doctor's fingers pressed against James' cheek bone and jaw, James would pull back.

"That's pretty tender, huh?"

"Yes, sir."

The doctor couldn't help but notice the unusual look of James' cheek bone. "Think there's something else going on here besides a bruised face. We need to get a CAT scan," he said to the nurse.

I need to call my brother. That was only one of many thoughts that went through James' mind at that moment.

"We'll talk some more after you return from x-ray," said Dr. Swanson as he patted James' leg and turned to go.

"I need to call my brother."

"That can wait. I need to get you to x-ray to see what might be going on inside that head of yours." He left the cubicle.

James looked at Rocky with pleading eyes and pointing to his jacket lying on the chair, "Get my phone and call Stephen."

"Sure 'nuf. I'm assuming you have his number listed under Stephen Pearce?"

James gently nodded his head.

Just then an orderly pulled back the curtain and wheeled in a gurney followed by a second man. "Mr. Pearce?"

"Yes."

"We're gonna take ya for a ride," said the orderly as James was scooted onto the gurney and they were out of there in no time.

Rocky made the call to Stephen and then just sat there in the chair shaking his head, his mouth pursed as he thought, *how I wished I'd made him put on that seatbelt. But, it's too late now to cry over spilt milk.* He let out a big sigh of disgust. *Sure hope he comes through this okay.* Feeling antsy, he got up and walked outside the cubicle. Back inside again, he sat straight up in his chair with a sudden moment of realization, *I need to call James' wife and let her know he's been hurt. Her number should be in his cell phone.*

Chapter 9

Paul pulled his car into the parking lot at the hospital, quite anxious to see his mother. They no sooner entered the front door into the lobby, when they saw Sonja. She did not see them at first, as her eyes were fixed on the makeshift carrier in her hands that held three cups of *fresh* hot coffee.

"Sonja."

She looked to her right and then to her left and until her brother called out again, "Sonja" did she notice them behind her.

"Paul. Sandy." They hugged her. "It's so good to see you. I'm getting coffee for those of us in the ICU waiting room. Could I get you some coffee?"

"No, thanks. We had some just a little while ago. How's Mother?"

Sonja started for the elevator with her brother and sister-in-law at her side. "There's been no change. Stephen keeps reassuring us that the coma is better for her if she has any brain injuries, as it gives it time to heal. I just want to see her open her eyes and call my name. I know that sounds selfish, but that's how I feel."

Paul put his arm around his sister's waist, careful not to bump her arm holding the coffee. "Hey, Sis, that's not selfish. We all want the same thing."

Just as the three were ready to enter the elevator, they heard someone calling, "Sonja."

They turned to see Jeff, Sonja's husband.

"Hi, sweetie," said Sonja. She smiled, unbelievably happy to see her husband.

They exited the elevator on the second floor and saw Gordon and Trisha walking from the ICU ward.

"How's Mom?" asked Sonja.

"No change," said Gordon.

"I'm taking the coffee into the waiting room," said Sonja. "Who's in with Mom now?"

"Stephen and Marianne. They said they'd stay ten minutes and then give someone else ample time with Mom. Paul and Sandy, you need to take your turn next." Gordon wasn't trying to be in command, just fair.

Paul looked around the ICU waiting room and asked Cassie, "Any of the grandkids been here?"

"No. They're all working. They've been notified, so I'm sure they'll be here after work."

Stephen's cell phone vibrated in his pocket. He stepped out of the ICU ward to check the number and saw that it was James calling him.

"James. Where are you?"

"Um . . . ah . . . this is Rocky, a friend of James. Your brother is here in the ER."

"Here? You mean here in the Middleton hospital?"

"Yes. My plane blew a tire on landing and James hit his head on the dashboard. He asked me to call you to let you know that he's here in the ER."

"I'll be right there." Stephen pushed the 'off' key and stood there for a moment trying to wrap his mind around that news. He then walked back in beside Velma's bed and whispered to his wife, "I've got to go downstairs to the ER. James was in an accident and he's hurt." He turned and left.

On his way to the elevator he stopped at the waiting room to share his news with the family.

"Hey, you guys. James is downstairs in the ER."

"What?" Cassie asked. "Why?"

"He was hurt when his friend's plane had an accident."

"Is he okay?" asked Gordon.

"Don't know. I'm headin' down there, now."

"Me, too," said Gordon.

"Wait for me," said Cassie.

Stephen turned toward Paul, "Why don't you and Sandy go in next to see Mom."

Feeling that her husband needed that time alone with his mother, Sandy said, "Paul, you go ahead. I'll be in there in a few minutes."

The three siblings headed out the door, leaving the sisters-in-law in the waiting room. Riding down in the elevator, Stephen said, "This beats all. Now we have James to be concerned with. Hope he's okay."

The three were shown to James' ER cubicle, but no one was in the bed. "Lookin' for James?" asked a voice that came from behind them.

"Yes. We're his family."

"I'm Rocky, James' friend. Your brother is having x-rays taken at the moment."

The three of them decided to just hang around for a few minutes, hoping that James would soon return to the ER.

Marianne and Trisha were spending their waiting time with Sandy catching up on all the news from her family and what was going on in Walla Walla. A nurse had made a fresh pot of coffee, so the three sipped on their cups of coffee while they talked.

"I heard Cassie say that she was glad her Dad was not here now to witness this trauma to her mom. He could not have handled the situation at all. His heart would be broken, not being able to *fix* whatever was wrong with his wife," said Trisha.

"Stephen is a lot like that," said Marianne. "Whenever I'm sick, he becomes irritated because the situation is completely out of his hands. He paces and when the kids still lived at home, I could hear him yelling at them, seemingly over nothing."

"I think that's a male trait," said Sandy. "They are sure different from women. When I get to Heaven, I plan to ask God, 'Why did you make men the way you did?'" The two laughed at her revealing that story, mostly because, they, too had thought something similar in the past.

"I wouldn't want Paul any other way," said Sandy. "I really got a gem for a husband when I asked him to marry me."

"You what? You asked him?" questioned Marianne.

"Yup. He had hemmed and hawed around several times starting to ask me to marry him, but never got right down to business. So . . . one evening as he was driving me home after a date, I said, 'Paul, we've dated now for over a year. We've talked about the kinds of furniture we like and where we'd like to live, but you've never come right out and said, will you marry me. How come?'

"He shook his head from side to side until I thought it would fall off, and then he took a big deep breath and said, 'You don't understand. I just . . . well, I just . . .'

"Well, I decided if I was ever going to hear him say he wanted to marry me then I'd have to ask him. 'Paul, will you marry me?' He pulled the car over to the curb, grabbed me around the shoulders and gave me the biggest bear hug that almost took the breath out of me, all the while saying, 'Yes. Yes. Yes.'"

The two sisters-in-law laughed out loud right along with Sandy.

"All along, he had been putting it off because he was afraid to approach my father to ask for my hand in marriage. I know that's old fashioned according to today's younger generation, but Paul's upbringing made him the gentle moral man he is today. He was not afraid of my dad, who was a state patrolman, but he was scared that he might say 'no' to him."

When she finished her story, she said, "I think I'll go see how Paul's doing in there with his mom."

The other two spent the next little while alone chatting or telling story after story about themselves and their spouses.

In the ICU ward, Sandy walked in to find Paul holding on to his mom's hand and carrying on a one-sided conversation with her.

Sandy sat quietly down on the opposite side of the bed from Paul, allowing him to continue to speak to his mother. She turned quickly as she saw someone enter the ward. It was Velma's pastor. He recognized Paul and then made his way over to Velma's bed.

Paul stood to greet the visitor. "Thank you for coming."

"I wanted to come earlier, but I had a funeral to preach at two this afternoon."

"I'm just pleased that you're here now."

"I can't tell you, Paul, how many times over the years that this woman has been there for me. I was in shock when I heard the details of your mother's accident. How is she?"

"She's still unconscious."

Pastor Simpson moved to the other side of the bed to greet Sandy. He had met her on several occasions when the couple had come to Middleton for some family event, but he really didn't know her that well. They shook hands.

Sandy continued to hold the pastor's hand. She said, "Pastor, thank you for being here, not only for Paul's mother, but for all of us. Right now we are at an unusual juncture. She has always been there for us, just as you also mentioned, but we've never had the occasion to really be there for her.

"It reminds me of the story in the Bible about the woman who broke the alabaster box of perfume over Jesus. It was the only way she knew how to express her love for Him. He had shown His love every day of His life for others, but now He was on the way to His death on the cross and this was one time someone was there to show their love for Him."

"Beautifully said," remarked the pastor, still holding Sandy's hand. She dropped her hand and wrapped her arms around the pastor and gave him a big hug. She would never really know just how much that meant to him at that moment.

Pastor Simpson was a widower. His wife of fifty-five years had gone home to be with the Lord a little over a year earlier. He seemed lost for so many, many months afterwards. Eva was not able to conceive and therefore they had no children.

During his time of grieving, he even contemplated giving up his pastorate, believing he couldn't handle it without Eva at his side. After all, he was seventy-nine-years-old and he had even mentioned to the church board at one time that he should retire. The men on the board talked him out of it, telling him that he still had the fire of God in him and they needed that in their pastor.

Velma Pearce had been the one person in his congregation who he felt really understood his loneliness. She had managed to survive so gracefully after the loss of her own spouse. He observed Velma's life after she was widowed and admired the way in which she carried on with her life. *She's a good example for all of us*, he had often said to his wife. At this very moment his heart went out to her children as they stood in loving vigil over their mother.

Something strange began to take place within Pastor Simpson as he stood looking down at Velma's almost lifeless body. He had never sensed before that he had more feelings for this woman than just as her pastor. He had to admit, though, that vague thoughts in that area had crossed his mind in the past couple of months, but he had dismissed them, thinking, *you ol' fool. You're too old to start a relationship with any woman.*

But, now the depth of his friendship with her became clear. He closed his eyes and silently prayed, *O, Lord, this precious woman is in need of her Savior's healing touch. Minister to her as You did to the son of the widow woman in Luke's Gospel where You said to her son, 'Young man, I say unto thee, Arise.' He was healed. Do that again, Lord. Please, do that again.* He opened his eyes and reached out his hands toward Paul and Sandy. As they held hands, the pastor prayed a prayer of healing faith over his dear sister-in-Christ.

Tears poured from the eyes of Paul and Sandy, tears of joy that God was completely in control of Velma's situation. The tears also were shed for the preciousness of the pastor's prayer for the family. Paul sensed a burst of strength flow into him – a very unusual feeling. He wiped his eyes and thanked the pastor for the prayer.

Then he said, "Pastor, when I was home on leave from the Army I wrote in the fly-leaf of my bible a scripture that you used as your text in your sermon that Sunday morning. I had been in trouble a couple of times during the past few months and I had recanted for my sins during the opening prayer that Sunday morning. Then you shared from the Old Testament, Nahum 1:7."

"Do you mean you still remember what it says?" asked his wife.

Paul nodded his head. "It says, 'The Lord is good, a strong hold in the day of trouble; and He knoweth them that trust in Him.' Your message that morning using that very scripture was just the beginning of turning my life around. Those words stayed with me while I served in the Army and again on my job at the prison."

The pastor humbly smiled and said, "Thank you, Paul, for sharing that with me." He turned to leave the room and said, "Now, young people, I have an appointment that I must attend to. I'll check in with your mother later today."

He left wanting that time to be reserved for Velma's family.

On his way home from the hospital, Pastor Simpson drove slower than usual, stunned by the revelation of his feelings for Velma. At his age, he would never have envisioned a relationship with another woman. His wife had been the love of his life and help-mate in his ministry to such an extent that when she died, he felt lost and overwhelmed. Only with prayer and attending to the constant spiritual needs of others did he get through that period of time.

He pulled his SUV over to the curb; his hands firmly gripped the steering wheel as he prayed, "Lord! Is it possible that I could have a life with someone else? I'm eighty, Lord. But then, you already know that.

"If I'm to ever remarry, my choice would be Velma. My wife and I always felt a kindred spirit with her. Oh, Lord, I'm . . . I'm utterly flabbergasted at this moment at this surprising turn of events. Sometimes we don't know ourselves as much as we thought we did.

"Lord, help me now to keep my head on straight, my heart clean and my mind headed in the right direction. I pray this in Jesus' precious name. Amen."

He sat for another few moments before he could put the car in gear and continue on his way home. As he drove he couldn't help but think of the widows and single women in his church who began to pay more attention to him after his beloved wife had passed away.

He shook his head and grinned when he thought about how Ms. Higgenbottom brought him her county-fair award-winning cherry pie the day after his wife's funeral. Then there was Widow Chambers who giggled each time she shook hands with him and in a coy manner invited him to dinner at her place after church. He kindly thanked her for the invitation, but said that he already had plans. The plan was - that he would never go to her place for dinner. He smirked as he remembered the many invitations and food gifts he had received from women since his wife's death.

With Velma, it had been different. She treated him before and after his wife's death in the same caring way that any parishioner would respect and love their pastor. No hidden agenda.

Now, as he pulled into his driveway he turned off the engine and just sat there. He looked up into the heavens and said, "Oh, Eva. I miss you so. I knew I could talk anything over with you. You were always a good sounding board. Am I being a crazy ol' fool?" He leaned his head down on the steering wheel as tears came into his eyes at the thought of his beloved wife.

Chapter 10

At the police precinct, Sergeant Jackson finished the last piece of paperwork that had to be completed before the end of his shift. He scooted back his chair, his hands now behind his head and his chin raised up. He was thinking about Tony Ramirez. *At his age, Tony could turn in two different directions. He can either be all that he can be or throw all caution to the wind. Think I'll give his mom a call and see if it's all right that I pick him up and take him over to the hospital. He seemed deeply concerned about the old lady.*

He scooted his chair back toward his desk and reached in the drawer for the phone book. "Hmm. Convenience stores," he said out loud as he checked the yellow pages. "She said it was the one over on 11th Street. Ah, here it is - 645-2121."

"Who you talkin' to, Jackson?" said one of his co-workers.

"To the moon." He picked up the phone to punch in the numbers and then waited. "May I speak to Consuela Ramirez, please."

"Speaking."

"Mrs. Ramirez, this is Sergeant Jackson. I met you at your apartment this morning."

"Oh, yes sir. What can I do for you?"

"I'd like to go by and pick up Tony and take him over to the hospital to meet the lady who was injured this morning, if that's all right with you. He seemed tormented about what he'd done to her, so I thought it might help him to visit with her."

"Um . . . I . . . I guess that would be all right. I'll call him and tell him that you're coming for him. When will that be?"

"I'll be leaving the police station in about fifteen minutes."

"All right, Sgt. Jackson."

"I'll only keep him away from home for just a short while."

"Thank you, sir."

Sgt. Jackson scooted his chair back one more time, leaning heavily into its back. He shook his head *Yup, need to get him over there. He's had too much time on his hands by himself today. That's not good.* He reached over and put the telephone book back in the drawer and then took a couple of minutes to affix his signature to some reports. Finished for the day, he got his hat and strode to the door.

The expected knock on the door of the Ramirez's apartment was quickly answered by Tony. "Hi."

"Hi, Tony. Your mom told you I was coming?"

"Yes, sir."

"Didja get your science project finished."

"Yes, sir."

"Okay," Sgt. Jackson said exuberantly. "Ready to go over to the hospital?"

"Yes, sir."

The ride to the hospital was quiet, with Sgt. Jackson doing the talking that was done. Tony, on the other hand, was very anxious. It became obvious to the seasoned cop that the young boy was quite uneasy.

As the police car pulled into the hospital parking lot, Tony said, "What if she dies?"

"Oh, Tony, let's not think negatively. We have to think in a positive vein until we know all the facts. Let's go, fella."

Tony had a hard time keeping up with Sgt. Jackson's long stride, almost running to stay up with him.

Inside the lobby, Sgt. Jackson asked the receptionist for the room number of Mrs. Pearce. He knew her name as he had looked it up on the police report prior to leaving the precinct.

"She's in ICU on the second floor."

"Thank you." The two headed for the elevator. Arriving on the second floor Sgt. Jackson looked for a sign on the wall for the direction of the ICU ward and spotting it, pointed to the right, "This way."

They reached the nurses' station. "Is it possible to see Mrs. Pearce?"

"Are you family?"

"No, ma'am."

"I'm sorry, but only members of her immediate family are allowed in the ICU ward. Some of her family members are in the waiting room, if you'd like to go down there." She pointed to her right.

"Thank you, ma'am." Tony followed as Sgt. Jackson walked toward the waiting room.

Inside, everyone looked up as the uniformed policeman entered the room. He nodded politely at the people and then said, "I'm looking for the family of Mrs. Pearce."

Stephen stood up and said, "I'm her son."

"I was called to the scene after your mother's accident. This is Tony Ramirez, the young boy who was riding his bicycle and hit your mother. He's come to speak with her."

Tony was standing almost behind Sgt. Jackson for protection. He was afraid of what all those people might do to him for having hurt their mother.

Sgt. Jackson stepped aside and said, "Tony, this is Mrs. Pearce's son."

Stephen immediately put out his hand to shake hands with Tony. As soon as he said, "Young man," Tony shrank back again, afraid of what this man was going to say or do.

"Tony, I appreciate you coming to see my mother, but she's still unconscious."

With his head bent, Tony said, "I'm sorry, sir, for what I did to your mother. I didn't mean to hurt her."

"Tony, I heard that it was an accident and that you didn't do it on purpose. It's going to be okay."

"Is Mrs. Pearce going to be okay?" Tony asked.

"Well . . . we're not sure. Come over here and meet my family." He ushered Tony down the line of family members. After the last person, Stephen said, "We have another brother, but he's downstairs in the emergency room. He was injured in a plane accident on his way here to see our mother."

"I'm sorry. Will he be okay?"

"Right now they are checking him to see the extent of his injuries. Speaking of him, I'd better go back down there. First, though, Sgt. Jackson, may I have a word with you?"

"Sure."

"Out in the hallway?"

"Yes, sir." Turning to Tony, the policeman said, "Have a seat, son. I'll be right back."

Out in the hallway, Stephen asked Sgt. Jackson to share with him what he knew about the accident. When they were through talking, Stephen headed for the elevator and Sgt. Jackson walked back into the waiting room.

"Tony," said Sgt. Jackson, "since you won't be able to talk with Mrs. Pearce today, I think we'll leave and come back again tomorrow. Is that okay with you?"

"Yes, sir."

Sonja spoke up, "Sergeant, there's a phone here in the waiting room. Why don't you call to see if Mother is awake before you make another trip over here."

"Good idea. Thanks. Tony, let's go."

Velma's family said goodbye to Tony and again reassured him that they knew he didn't intentionally hurt their mother.

The two left the waiting room, Sgt. Jackson, sensing that the short visit was good for Tony – if only to see that Mrs. Pearce's family wasn't angry with him.

Chapter 11

James was wheeled back into the ER cubicle. The doctor had scheduled so many tests that his brothers and sister had decided to go back upstairs to the waiting room. They left a message for him with Rocky.

"So you've decided to rejoin the living?" was Rocky's response as James was helped up onto the bed.

"Yes. I've been twisted and turned and . . . everything else," said James, still speaking through his teeth.

"So?"

"Whatta ya mean, 'so'?"

"What've they told you?"

"Nothing."

"Your family was down here to see you. They left and went back upstairs since it was taking so long for your tests."

"Well, at least they know where I am."

"Yes."

Just then Dr. Swanson came in. He patted James' leg and said, "I've been down to talk with the radiologist and he verified that your cheek bone is fractured. I've called a surgeon to come down and take a look at those pictures and tell me what the next move should be."

"Oh, no," said James.

Stephen appeared in the cubicle. "Hey, brother, what's goin' on?"

Dr. Swanson turned toward Stephen and said, "He has a hard time talking, his right cheek bone is fractured. I'm waiting for the surgeon to come down to help determine what action we should take next."

"Wow. Brother, when you do something, you do it with flair."

"Not funny," retorted James. "How's Mother?"

"Still unconscious. They won't do surgery on her broken hip for a day or so, hoping she'll come to in the meantime."

"Everybody here?"

"Yup. Grandkids haven't showed up yet, as they're all working. I notified Aunt Mary in San Antonio. She, of course, couldn't make the trip since her rheumatoid arthritis has her too crippled up. I dropped by the nursing home on my way here to let Uncle Charles know about the accident."

James opened his mouth to speak, but groaned as a sharp pain shot through the right side of his face.

"Just lay there and be quiet, for a change," said Stephen, with a big grin. "Those prosecutors in Portland would be happy to see that you're not able to talk."

"You're so funny," James was able to mumble.

Stephen turned to Rocky, "What happened to him?"

"Well . . . it's like this. Your stubborn brother decided not to refasten his seatbelt and when the plane landed, a tire blew, throwing him against the dashboard. Nothing I could've done to prevent it. I was too busy trying to get the plane stopped and kept upright."

Stephen turned back to James and grinned, "So, the stubborn one in the family got his just desserts."

"Hey. You aren't supposed to kick a guy when he's down," James was able to say. While growing up, James was the one person who could keep the family laughing. He had a sense of humor that could make an old scrooge smile.

Stephen touched the toes on his brother's left foot and said, "You know me well enough to know I'm not making light of your accident. Hey, brother, since only two people at-a-time can be in the room with Mom, the others will be coming down here soon to see you."

Dr. Swanson interrupted. "We'll probably be putting him into a room in just a short while."

With that, Dr. Swanson left to go back to the x-ray lab to meet with the surgeon and radiologist.

He had no sooner left when Sonja, Jeff and Marianne appeared in the cubicle. James tried to lift his head to welcome them, but eased back down.

Stephen spoke up, "James, just stay down. You could possibly do more damage when you move around."

"What kind of damage is there?" asked Sonja.

"He has a shattered cheek bone," her brother replied. Turning and pointing toward Rocky, he said, "Oh, by the way, this is Rocky, James' friend and pilot."

They all shook hands and greeted Rocky.

"What happened to James," Sonja said, addressing Rocky.

"Ah, let me tell it," said Stephen. "Seems our stubborn brother neglected to fasten his seatbelt and he went flying into the dashboard."

"Oh," said Sonja. She turned to James, "Bless your heart, James. You've always learned your lessons the hard way. Sure hope they can fix you up."

"Folks," said Rocky, addressing the Pearce family. "Now, that he's in your hands, I need to head back out to the airport to see if they've been able to fix my plane. If not, I'll need to get a room for the night."

He walked over to James' bed, "Friend, I'm really sorry for what you've had to go through. Let me know the results, okay? I'll check in with my insurance company as soon as I get back to Portland. See you there. Oh, by the way, I called Wanda and let her know. She's catching the next plane up here."

"Thanks, Rocky. You're a good friend."

Stephen put out his hand to shake Rocky's hand and said, "Listen, if you have to stay the night, just give me a call and you can stay at our place. No sense in getting a hotel room."

"Thanks, but no thanks. You folks have enough to be concerned with. I should be able to find someplace to lay my head for a few hours."

"If you change your mind, here's my phone number," said Stephen as he fished in his pocket for something to write on.

"Here," said Sonja, handing her brother a piece of scrap paper from her purse.

"Thanks, Sis. You women carry everything but the kitchen sink in those purses of yours." He wrote the number down and handed it to Rocky.

"Thanks, Stephen. Good to meet all of you," were Rocky's final words as he turned and left.

Upstairs in the ICU ward, Gordon and Trisha sat on each side of Velma's bed, with Trisha reading to Velma from the Book of Psalms. Gordon remembered that the Psalms were some of his mother's favorite portions of the Bible. Trisha had picked Psalms 37, one of her own favorite passages.

"Mama, listen to this," said Trisha, "Psalms 37:3 says. *Trust in the Lord, and do good; so shalt thou dwell in the land, and verily thou shalt be fed.* Verse 4 says, *Delight thyself also in the Lord, and he shall give thee the desires of thine heart.* Mama, verse 5 is really good. It says, *Commit thy way unto the Lord; trust also in him; and he shall bring it to pass.*"

Gordon broke in, "Mama, did you hear that? I really think that was written just for your six children – for this very day." Tears had formed in his eyes while he was talking, as that passage had truly ministered to him.

Trisha passed him the small tissue box from Velma's night stand. "Here, sweetheart."

He just smiled as he wiped his eyes.

"Gordon, we've been in here longer than we should have. We need to go so someone else can have visiting time."

"You're right." He leaned down and kissed his mother's forehead. "I'll be back in just a little while, Mama. You be a good girl, do you hear me?" He closed his eyes momentarily and then stood up to leave.

Consuela Ramirez turned the key in the lock of her apartment and went in. "Tony. I'm home." He wasn't in the living room or kitchen, so she headed down the hall to his room. "Tony. You okay?"

He was lying on his back on his bed and lifted his head when his mother entered the room. "Yes, Mama."

Consuela sat down on the edge of Tony's bed and put her hand on his shoulder. "What's wrong?"

"Mama, what if that lady never comes to?"

"Tony, one of the things I learned from Father Gomez is that we must have hope. He said, 'Hope expects and faith accepts.' That means until the lady gets better, we must hope, or in other words *believe* that she will come to and be able to go home soon. If that isn't God's plan for her, then we must have the faith to accept His plan. Do you understand what I'm saying?"

"I think so."

"Okay. Just remember the lady in your prayers tonight and believe that she will be okay."

"Mama, her name is Mrs. Pearce. Sgt. Jackson told me that."

"Oh. Okay. Pray for Mrs. Pearce. I will, too.

"We'll go see her tomorrow, but only if your homework is done." She gave him a kiss on his cheek and went to her bedroom to change into her nightgown and chenille robe.

Chapter 12

Velma's family waited impatiently for their mother's condition to improve. It was now nearing dinner time, so two couples at a time went downstairs to the cafeteria.

Stephen and Marianne had gone to the third floor surgery ward to be with James. The surgeon, radiologist and ER doctor had earlier concluded their findings of James' fractured cheek and had decided that surgery needed to be performed in the morning.

James' dinner tray had been brought in, which held only soft food that he could ingest easily without having to chew.

"Boy, look what you've got there, brother - yogurt, Jell-O and let's see what's under this lid – ah, broth. My, what a he-man-sized dinner."

"Hey, don't make me laugh. It hurts. Anything to drink?"

"Sorry, James, but the piece of paper on your tray says no caffine. Do you want your head raised a little?"

James nodded gingerly.

Stephen's cell phone started to pulse. He pulled it from his pocket and saw on the screen that Cassie was calling him.

"Hey, Sis, what's up?"

"Stephen, I was with Mother when she made some terrible gasping sounds. She didn't open her eyes, but her chest rose up and then she lay back down. The alarm on the monitor she was hooked up to went off, which brought three nurses and the crash-cart to Mother's bedside. They asked me to leave. I'm standing outside the door that goes into the ward and I'm so scared."

"I'll be right there." Stephen told James that Cassie needed him, not telling his brother the whole story. Instead of waiting for the elevator, Stephen took the stairs, two steps at a time. He rushed to Cassie's side as she waited at the door of the ward. The critical care nursing staff was still working on Velma.

"Stephen. She can't die. Please tell me she's not going to die."

"Cassie, get a hold of yourself. Right now we need to remember that Mom is in God's Hands," Stephen said, trying to reassure his sister. As a middle-school teacher and the adult Sunday school teacher, he has had experience in dealing with family trauma. He had a gift for knowing how to calm people down.

"Cassie, go to the waiting room and tell the others what's happening. They may want to go pray in the chapel."

"Okay." Reluctantly, she headed for the waiting room.

Stephen continued his vigil at the door. In what seemed like minutes, but were only just a few seconds, two of the three nurses opened the double doors and wheeled out the crash-cart.

"Is she okay?"

"You'll need to discuss that with her doctor. There's a nurse with her and the doctor is on his way."

"May I go in and see her?"

"No. You need to wait until the doctor has been in there with her."

Stephen took his time going to the waiting room only to find it empty. He turned back, and as he did, Cassie was getting off the elevator.

"I couldn't stay down there. I couldn't even keep my mind on praying. Have they said anything?"

"No. The doctor should be here at any moment."

The two took their positions beside the double doors, waiting for any word on their mother's condition. A doctor rushed past them and into the ward. As he did, Cassie tried to see what she could when he opened the doors. All she could determine was that a nurse was standing at her mother's bedside.

A few minutes later, the doctor came out and asked, "Are you family to Mrs. Pearce?"

"Yes, we're her children."

"We're affixing a heart monitor to your mother and she'll have an oxygen mask put on her, also. Since she is still unconscious, we can't ask her any questions. We'll monitor your mother's condition very closely." He pointed to the monitors lined up at the nurse's station and then continued, "A monitor is checking your mother's heart rate, blood pressure, oxygen saturation and temperature. With this latest situation, a nurse will closely watch to observe any changes made in your mother's heart rhythm. I will notify the cardiologist on duty to examine your mother."

Cassie turned momentarily to observe the wide window whereby the ICU staff could watch the individuals on the ward. Then she turned back to the doctor.

"May we see her?"

"Not right now. Please be patient."

"All right. Thank you, doctor." Stephen turned to Cassie and said, "I'll go down to the chapel and tell the others what we've learned. Will you stay here and watch for the heart specialist?"

"Yes," Cassie said, in a firm voice, implying she wouldn't have it any other way.

Some chairs were lined up against the wall across from the nurse's station and Cassie decided she needed to sit down. This latest event had left her quite shaken. She kept a watchful eye down the hall for the cardiologist to appear. Her left knee began to pump up and down, a sign of anxiety, as she sat there wondering what was keeping that doctor from attending to her mother.

Her mind quickly turned to James and wondered what was taking place with him. *I can't believe we have both mother and James in this hospital. I'm so glad that there are five other kids in the family besides me to look after the two of them. If there had only just been me, I would've gone crazy trying to run from floor to floor checking on the both of them. Good thing Mom and Dad had six of us.* She smiled. It had been hours since she had anything to smile about today.

The elevator chimed, the door opened and out came a doctor dressed in his usual white physician's coat. *Sure hope that's the cardiologist.* She wanted to get up and grab his arm as he passed by, but only watched as he went into the ICU ward. She could not sit there any longer, but went over to the desk to ask if that was the heart specialist.

A nurse smiled and said, "Yes. He's a good doctor. Best in the Northwest. He could've had a position in any big hospital in the country, but he chose Middleton. His elderly parents live in the area and he wanted to be close by should they ever have any heart problems. He's a very caring man."

Cassie turned and went back to sit down and wait some more. The elevator chimed again and out came Stephen. "Doctor show up, yet?"

"Yes. He's in there with Mama now." She noticed that she had been calling her mother, 'Mama', which she hadn't done in years.

"Cassie, I'm going to call Pastor Simpson so that he can get in touch with some of the people in Mom's Sunday school class to be praying." He pulled out his cell phone and scrolled down to the pastor's name.

The pastor didn't answer at first, and Stephen shrugged his shoulders as the seconds ticked by.

"He may be at the church," said Cassie.

"Oh, he's an up-to-date clergyman, he has a cell phone." He smiled at her. "Oh, by the way, Paul went up to the third floor to be with James. We decided that he shouldn't tell James at this point about Mom's condition. James is preparing his own mind about the surgery he'll have in the morning. Say, when is Wanda supposed to arrive?"

"Not sure. I was told that she would take a taxi from the airport over here."

"Ah. Pastor, this is Stephen Pearce. I wanted to let you know that our mother has had a slight stroke or a possible heart-attack – not really sure at this point-in-time." The two talked for another minute or so and then they ended the call.

≈

When Pastor Simpson had answered Stephen's call, he was quite shocked to hear the latest news about Velma. He had gone to the church to work on his sermon for the coming Sunday. When he hung up the receiver, he immediately shoved his books, Bible and notebook to the back of his desk. He opened a side drawer on his desk to get out the phone list of the Sunday school class that Velma teaches. He would call one person and they would in turn call the others. His hand shook as he punched in the phone number on his desk phone. *Oh, dear Lord. Please don't let her die.* "Oh, hello. Hello. Ah . . . this is Pastor . . . ah . . . Pastor Simpson." He was having such hard time concentrating. "I called you earlier about Velma being in the hospital. Well . . . um . . . now she's had a possible heart attack. Please call the others to be praying."

The party on the other end of the line thanked him for the call and that ended it.

He sat back in his leather chair, took a deep breath and released it slowly. He was quiet for a moment as he reflected on the revelation earlier in the day of his feelings for Velma. He sat back up with a start knowing he must get over to the hospital. Velma's children would need him now. When he stood up, he became well aware that this latest news had upset him more than he realized. His legs were shaking.

He sat back down and called his much younger sister, Nellie. "Nellie, can you give me a ride over the hospital?"

"Are you sick?"

"No, Nellie. I need to get over there. Velma Pearce has had a possible heart attack. I'm a little shook up about it and I don't feel that I should drive."

"Oh. Sure. I'll be right there."

"Nellie?"

"Yes."

"I'm at the church."

"Oh. Okay."

Thankfully, she only lived two streets away, so he put on his suit jacket and slowly made his way to the front porch of the church to wait for her.

The pastor got in his sister's car and said, "Thanks, Sis. I hope I didn't take you away from anything important."

"Well, you did," she responded. "I was just about to watch Wheel of Fortune when you called. Don't know if I can forgive you for that." She grinned and glanced at him.

He knew she was kidding, as she had been a big kidder all her life. She brought a lot of joy into his broken heart when his wife passed away.

"By the way, Brother, I grabbed the evening paper off the porch. A quick scan of the front page told of Velma's accident. It seems that a newspaper reporter had been listening to the police scanner and overheard talk about an older woman being knocked down by a bicycle."

"Nothing seems to get past a reporter."

"I know. But, hopefully the article on Velma will help to spread the word that she needs prayer."

"Never thought about it in that way, Sis." He picked up the folded newspaper and saw the article right away. They rode in silence the rest of the way to the hospital, only a couple of miles from the church.

≈

Cassie and Stephen stood once again beside Velma's bed after having been allowed back into the ICU ward. Velma was as still as she had been before. Cassie looked down at her mother, not knowing just what to think at the moment.

"Cassie," whispered Stephen, "we need to go and let two of the others to come and be with Mother?"

"Yeah. You're right."

When Stephen informed the others in the ICU waiting room that they could go see Velma, Gordon and Paul, who were sitting closest to the door, were the first two to get to their feet. "Guess Paul and I will go for just a very few minutes," said Gordon.

"We'll be right back," stated Paul.

The two men walked quickly toward the ICU ward just as Cassie was exiting through the double doors. They each gave their sister a hug, with no words being necessary.

Standing on each side of the bed, the two men looked down at their mother, who looked more frail than they had ever seen her before. Both men couldn't stand the looks of the IV needle in her arm, an oxygen mask on her face, heart monitor wires affixed to different places on her upper body and a feeding tube. She didn't look like the strong, vibrant woman they had always known.

"Mom, Gordon and I are here to see you," Paul said, as he leaned closer to her head. "All of your kids are here. Isn't that great? We're just waitin' for you to open your eyes so that we can all go home and have a party." Paul raised his eyes to look at his brother and then shook his head. It was so difficult for the sons, as they so desperately wanted to do something to help their mother.

"Hey, Gordon, why don't you sing something for Mother?"

"What? Me, sing?"

"Yeah, you. I've heard you sing before. If I remember right, you have a tenor voice, don't you?"

"You've got a bad memory, Paul. I'm a tenor alright. But when I sing, *ten-or eleven* people get up and leave."

"You're so funny, Gordon. Did you hear that, Mom? He's the Bill Cosby of the Pearce family. Did you know, Mother, that I sang a solo in church last Sunday? Yup, I sure did - so low that no one could hear me."

"Ha. Ha. Ha," said Gordon, with a big grin on his face.

Paul looked at his brother and said, "Let's go, Gordon, and let two more come in."

"Right." Gordon bent down and kissed his mother's forehead and whispered, "I love you, Mom." Then he left the room.

Paul followed his brother after saying to his mom, "We've prayed and we're all believing that you're going to be just fine." He turned to leave the room as Sonja and Trisha were making their way into the ward. Paul touched each of their hands as he passed by them as an expression of love and support.

When Paul walked into the waiting room, Pastor Simpson and his sister, Nellie, were there sitting with the Pearce family. He excused himself to go in and see Velma. Thankfully, clergymen are allowed into the ICU ward at any time. His sister, Nellie, stayed with the family.

After spending a few quiet moments with Velma in the presence of Sonja and Trisha, Pastor Simpson sensed that he should go up to the third floor to see James. In the elevator, the old gentleman thought *I haven't seen James since he went away to college. I don't know if I'll even recognize him.* He chuckled as he thought *I've got grey hair, thirty more pounds and a wrinkled face since he saw me last - it'll be a wonder if he'll recognize me.*

The visit was short and sweet as James was sound asleep. The pastor reached down and laid his hand on James' hand and prayed silently.

———

Chapter 13

Catherine Williams put down the newspaper and went out to the garage where her husband was tinkering with his car. "John, Mrs. Pearce has been injured and is in the hospital."

"What?" he said as he picked up a rag to wipe off his hands.

"It was in this evening's paper. Samantha will be so upset. She dearly loves that lady."

"I hope this doesn't put a damper on the upcoming court case. Samantha will be lost without Mrs. Pearce at her side."

"I never thought about that. I need to go and talk with Samantha right now. Tomorrow I'll call the prosecuting attorney's office and see how this may affect the court case." She turned to go back in the house and then yelled over her shoulder, "Dinner will be ready in about twenty-minutes! I'll call you when it's time to eat."

"Thanks, sweetheart. I just want to check the oil."

Catherine and John, now in their late forties, had become foster parents to Samantha. She had been placed in their home after several reports of abuse in her own home. The court had appointed Velma Pearce as guardian ad litem for Samantha.

Velma Pearce had applied to be a volunteer as a guardian ad litem or advocate for the CASA/GAL program soon after her husband, George, had passed away, some years earlier.

She had obtained all the information she could before putting in her application. She had always loved kids and could not think of a better use of her time than to save a child from further harm by an adult.

A guardian ad litem appointee is a person appointed by a judge to speak for a child when that child is a part of a court case due to no fault of his own. Although such matters are usually heard in Juvenile Court, charges will have been filed against the parents either in civil or criminal court showing abuse or neglect of the child.

The State's Department of Children's Services will take temporary custody of the child until the parent or parents have proven to the court that they have completed certain requirements and are capable of providing the child with a safe, stable home.

In such cases, the court may appoint a guardian ad litem to represent the child's best interests in court. This guardian ad litem (GAL) or court appointed special advocate (CASA) may be an attorney, a mental health professional, or any person over the age of twenty-one with a clean arrest record and who has completed the required training.

Although the State takes immediate temporary custody of a child in this situation, appropriate housing is sought, preferably with a relative. Only if no such placement can be found, will a child be put in the foster care system.

Regardless of where the child lives, the GAL or CASA will visit all persons involved in the child's life. Since they are appointed by court order, they are given access to all educational, medical or other reports regarding the child. A report is submitted to the judge at each court appearance. This helps the judge make decisions regarding the child's best interests. These volunteers have the time and the interest to fully investigate the child's past and present life. They work with the State's Department of Children's Services who, in turn, works with the parents in an effort to reunite the family.

≈

As Catherine Williams walked down the hall toward Samantha's bedroom, she regretted that she had to deliver bad news to her foster child. *She's had enough bad news in her short life* she thought as she knocked on Samantha's bedroom door.

Samantha kept her door shut, something she had been made to do in the house with her drug-dealing parents and uncle. Catherine and John had decided to let her continue that for a short while, but would wean her from her room when she became comfortable being around them.

"Come in."

Samantha was sitting on her bed doing homework. Catherine sat down beside her and made small talk at first and then shared the news about Velma's accident.

Samantha bowed her head, startled at the news. Tears formed in her eyes and then she lifted her head and asked, "Could we visit Mrs. Pearce at the hospital?"

Samantha so wanted the opportunity to see the woman who had become like a Grandmother to her. They had had long talks about school, friends and relatives.

"Can we go right now?"

"Whoa, girl. After dinner, we'll take a ride over to the hospital. In the meantime, think of some nice present that we can stop by and pick up on our way to see her. Any ideas?"

"Umm . . . would it be too silly to give her a picture of me? If she had that, she would know that I was thinking about her as she gets well."

"That's not silly, Samantha. I think Mrs. Pearce would like that very much. Let's ask Mr. Williams to take a picture of you right after dinner. You know how much he loves to take pictures. That camera has had a lot of use since he bought it. He could print out that picture and . . . I think . . . yes, I know I have a frame in the spare bedroom that you could put it in. Would that be okay?"

"Yes, ma'am. Is Mrs. Pearce going to be okay?"

"Well, sweetie, we'll find that out when we go over to the hospital. You get cleaned up and put on something real nice that would help to cheer up Mrs. Pearce."

Catherine left the bedroom and went back into the kitchen to put dinner on the table.

Samantha had been in a hospital only once before. That was when she was examined after she had been sexually assaulted by her uncle. That had been a traumatic situation that evening and one that Samantha probably would never forget. The fear that ran through that young child's being was almost inconceivable to an adult. She had no one but a female police officer there with her. Her parents, along with her uncle, had been arrested and taken to jail. Leaving the hospital that night, she was placed in temporary foster care until a more permanent foster family became available.

The next day, Velma Pearce had received the call from the court requesting that she be an advocate for Samantha.

Velma loved being able to help these children, but at the same time the unbelievable assault on the youngsters was heart-rending for her. *How could anyone deliberately harm a child?*

From the very first moment Velma saw Samantha she fell in love with her. Seeing her that first morning, she saw a frail, malnourished and unkempt child who was dragging behind her a dark green trash bag full of personal possessions. It appeared as though the temporary home had provided very little for her that first night. Velma had experienced that very same situation in the past where a child was just given only a bed and food until a foster home could be provided. Velma hated to see such inept care givers, but thankfully she saw only a very few of those incidences.

Velma saw in those big brown eyes of the young girl a fear that no child should have to endure. But she was so pleased to hear that the eleven-year-old was placed with the Williams.

The Williams had a long and honorable history for taking in children under the foster-care system. Their children were grown and married, leaving two bedrooms empty. The couple knew it would not always be easy because foster children have a lot of emotional baggage that is brought with them into the home. They knew they would have to cope at times with misunderstandings, fear and resentment, and of course misbehavior.

Velma's second visit with Samantha brought joy to the elderly lady's heart. The young girl's hair had been shampooed and her clothes were neat and clean. Samantha would stay with the Williams until after the trial of her uncle, who had been charged with sexual assault of a minor and drugs. Her parents were jailed on accessory to the sexual crime and also on drug possession and drug dealing charges. All three had been under the influence of drugs at the time of the arrest.

The abuse of Samantha would have continued had it not been for a neighbor who had called the police to report what appeared to be drug dealings at the house next door. They had watched over a period of time as unsavory-looking individuals streamed in and out of that house.

When the police arrived that night, they found Samantha in a clothes closet in a small back bedroom - weeping. Between sobs she was able to relate to them in broken sentences what her uncle had been doing to her. Immediately the three were arrested and taken to jail.

Samantha and her parents had only arrived in Middleton from Seattle a few months earlier. Samantha's mother and father had both lost their jobs due to drugs and had accepted an invitation from a 'druggy' brother to come and live with him in Middleton.

Samantha was not in school, spending her days in the drug-pervasive household. Meals were not prepared, so Samantha had to seek out any edible item in the house, which wasn't much. A few crackers and Styrofoam containers of left-over days-old fast-food in the refrigerator seemed to be the only items she could find to feed her growling empty stomach. The small nineteen-inch television was the only means of entertainment during the day and evening. It had been placed in her bedroom to keep her out of the daily, sometimes hourly, traffic that flowed through the living room.

Salt in an Unsavory World

≈

Now, as the Williams' stepped through the door of the hospital with Samantha, she grabbed onto Catherine's hand in a death grip and pulled herself as close as she could to her foster mother. They rode the elevator to the second floor with Samantha still holding Catherine's hand. Catherine knew of the young girl's experience at this hospital and could only guess at the humiliation her young charge had suffered.

At the nurse's station they were told that Mrs. Pearce could not have visitors, but they were politely directed to the waiting room where the Pearce family was still gathered.

Mr. Williams spoke up as they entered the room. "Are you Mrs. Pearce's family?"

Sonja said, "Yes," while the others just nodded their heads in affirmation.

"Um . . . I'm John Williams and this is my wife, Catherine." Putting his arm around the shoulders of Samantha, he continued, "This is Samantha. Mrs. Pearce is her appointed guardian ad litem."

Stephen stood up to greet them. "It's nice to meet you," said Stephen. "Let me introduce our family to you." After the introductions were made, Stephen moved closer to Mr. Williams and whispered, out of Samantha's hearing, "Mother has been unconscious since the accident and is in ICU. Only two family members can see her at a time."

"Is she going to be okay?"

Stephen shrugged his shoulders.

Stephen, a middle-school teacher, was used to talking with kids Samantha's age and sensed the need to put her at ease. "Aha, so you're Samantha. Our mother told us that she was helping with a pretty young girl named Samantha." He leaned down to where he was eyeball-to-eyeball with Samantha and said, "Mrs. Pearce is very sick right now, but we are all praying and believing God to make her well again. I know my mother would love to see you. But right now she's sound asleep and the doctors don't want us to disturb her."

Samantha hung her head. "Oh." She fumbled with the present she had in her hand, twisting and turning it. "Mister, would you give this to your mother?"

"I sure will."

"It's a picture of me. I wanted her to know that I'm thinking about her."

"What a nice gift," said Marianne as she leaned over her husband's shoulder to look at the photograph. She had been a part of her husband's classroom activities as long as she could remember. Turning to the others in the room she said, "Samantha brought Mother a picture of herself."

'Oh, how nice' and other comments could be heard from those in the room.

"We'll be going now. Would it be all right to call in the morning to see how your mother is doing?" asked Catherine.

"Of course," said Sonja. "Call here to the waiting room. A member of our family is always here. Let me write the phone number down for you so that you can call it direct."

"Thank you." The Williams' and Samantha said goodbye and left the room.

As soon as they had left, Sonja said to her siblings and their spouses, "Mama loves working with those kids. She told me in confidence one day about her first case. She said she was so nervous that day. You know, Mama. When she did something she wanted it to be done right. She wasn't sure of herself that day as she headed over to the house of her first case as a volunteer.

"The case had begun as a truancy case in the courts and ended with the children being taken away from the parents for unfathomable circumstances that the court was able to ascertain. The father went to prison and as far as Mama knows, the Mother is still drifting out there somewhere.

"Mama said that as she drove over there that first day – of course that's when she was still driving," she smiled and then continued, "she prayed the whole way there, asking God to help her to help those children. As soon as she stepped through the front door and saw those precious little children in the deplorable conditions that they had to live in a 'holy boldness' rose up in her. She said to herself, *With God's help, I'll do what I can to help these babies. They don't deserve this.*

"Mama fought long and hard, alongside the prosecuting attorney to keep those three kids from ever returning to their dad. After staying with foster parents for a period of time, they were happily adopted by a single mother of one son. She gave them every opportunity a child could ever want. Mama said that it was a lovely ending to an unspeakable beginning.

"Mama never divulged to me their names - she couldn't."

Paul spoke up, "Being a part of the CASA program has been such an essential part of Mama's life that has kept her happy and fulfilled."

Marianne spoke up, "Isn't it ironic that Mother spends her time working with youth, and then she is injured by a young boy?"

"There's a bigger picture here," speculated Stephen. "Right now we can't see what all God is doing through this tragedy. This is a wait and see situation."

Chapter 14

Catherine went into Samantha's bedroom to say goodnight and tuck her in. "I'm sorry you weren't able to see Mrs. Pearce tonight."

"I know. I hope she'll be better tomorrow so I can go and see her. Mrs. Williams, what did that man mean when he said to pray for Mrs. Pearce?"

"Ah . . . Samantha, have you ever gone to church?"

"No, ma'am. When we lived in Seattle, I walked past one every day on my way to school. I always wondered what they were doing in there."

"A church, Samantha, is where people go to honor God. You've heard of God, haven't you?"

"Yes, ma'am. When I went to school in Seattle, we said his name when we did the Pledge of Allegiance to the flag, but I didn't know who we were talking about. Oh, and . . . ah . . . I heard my mother and dad use that name when they were really mad."

Catherine gulped at that comment, knowing exactly what she meant. "You're right about the salute to the flag. We do honor God here in America for this wonderful country that He has given to us." Catherine continued on, doing her best to explain what it was like to be a Christian. Samantha began to yawn, so Catherine said, "Goodnight, little one. You've had a long day. We'll talk about this tomorrow. Okay?"

"Yes, ma'am. Goodnight."

Catherine started out the door when she heard, "Mrs. Williams."

"Yes."

"Why do bad things happen to nice people?"

"Well, Samantha, God never said in the Bible that he would keep us from having bad things happen to us. But, He did promise to always be there for us and help us through bad situations. You can be sure, Samantha that God is watching over Mrs. Pearce there in the hospital because her family prayed for God to help her. He'll be right there in the operating room tomorrow along with the doctors to make sure that she will be okay."

"Oh."

"I know it may be hard to understand, but that is where faith comes in. Faith is our belief that God will do what He says that He will do.

"Would you like us to pray right now for Mrs. Pearce?"

"Yes, ma'am."

"Samantha, close your eyes and I'll pray."

Afterward, Catherine walked up the hallway and realized that she hadn't prayed in a long time. *When we were first married and up until the time the kids all left home we were so faithful to attend church. But since then, we're probably what is called 'back-sliders'.*

That night, after going to bed, she cuddled up next to her husband and said, "Do you know what Samantha asked me tonight?"

"Not exactly, but it was probably something about Mrs. Pearce."

"Well, it was connected to our visit to see her, but . . . John, she asked me about prayer. She heard Mrs. Pearce's son say that they were praying for his mother. She wanted to know what that meant. I have to tell you that her question brought me up short. I really didn't know how to explain prayer to her because she told me she doesn't know who God is."

"Oh, my."

"Yeah. I kind of stammered around a little as I tried to explain God, church and prayer. It made me realize that we had left all that behind when the *empty-nest syndrome* took place in our lives."

"Sad to say, Catherine, but you're right. As soon as our last one left home, we started to take trips. We even went on a couple of cruises, believing that we could now stop having such a structured life. What happened is that we left God and church out of the equation. Then, when we got tired of all the running around, we delved into the foster care program and our busy life began all over again."

"Honey, Mrs. Pearce is very important to Samantha. If she were to die, Samantha would be lost without her. We definitely need to pray as Mrs. Pearce's son said they were doing. Pray that God will intervene and heal that dear lady."

"You're right."

Both lay back with their heads resting on their own pillows, with John asking Catherine to begin praying. They had, at one time, prayed together each night after getting in bed. It was a quiet time and a time alone where they could lift up the family problems to the Lord and also praise Him for the blessings that He had brought their way that particular day.

Catherine stalled for a moment. Guilt had risen up strong within her; she was almost afraid God wouldn't hear her as she prayed. "Lord, here we are. John and I need to first ask for your forgiveness for allowing everything and everyone to come before You. You still blessed us even though we were neglectful in our service to you and for that we are truly sorry.

"Tonight, we come to you, not for ourselves, but for Velma Pearce, a dear, dear lady whom Samantha loves so much. You already know that she needs healing, but the Bible tells us to *ask,* and so here we are - asking. She is such a special lady who loves You with her whole heart. John and I thank You now for what You're going to do for her. In Jesus' name we pray, Amen."

John began to pray, "Lord, help Samantha to understand who You are and why she needs Jesus in her heart and help us to convey that message to her. Samantha is a precious child and we ask that You look after her. Please implant Your wisdom into the mind of the prosecuting attorney and the judge whenever Samantha must go to court. She'll probably need a good home, and we ask that You raise up some fine people who will want her. Thank You, Lord. Amen."

In the ICU waiting room, just before dispersing for dinner, the Pearce family discussed among themselves where the out-of-towners were going to stay for the night.

Just then the door opened and in walked Wanda. "Hi, everyone."

The women all got up immediately to greet her, with the men following behind. The Pearce family knew very little about Wanda, as she and James had kept their distance for so many years - their lifestyle being so entirely different from the rest of the family. But right now, they were all together with their love and concern for Velma - and James.

"I just came from seeing James. I can't believe that my husband flew here to be with his mother and now he's waiting to go to the operating room in the morning."

"How's he doing?"

"He was sound asleep, but the nurse told me about the surgery."

Paul spoke up, "We left his room a little while ago as he had fallen asleep after being given some pain medication. The nurse said he would probably sleep for quite a while."

"You're right. His mouth was open and he was really sawing logs," James' wife quipped. "Of course, that's the way he always sleeps, sounding like a foghorn." That got a chuckle from everyone.

"Wanda, did you take a taxi from the airport?" asked Sonja.

"No. I picked up a rental car."

Attention was drawn to the door as two of the grandchildren, Rick and Cheri, came in. "Sorry that we couldn't get here earlier. How's Grandma?" asked Rick.

Wanda had not seen her husband's niece and nephew in years and was astonished at the fact she didn't recognize either of them.

After the introductions, she looked at the two young people and said, "You're adults now and you can stop calling me Aunt Wanda. Just Wanda will do."

Sandy turned away and she rolled her eyes. "She doesn't want anyone to think she's old enough to have nieces and nephews in their late twenties," she whispered to Trisha, who was sitting next to her, "Wanda hasn't changed any. She's still 'Ms. Highfalutin' as ever."

Trisha frowned and elbowed Sandy.

"Sorry. That was uncalled for," said Sandy.

It was decided that instead of going downstairs to eat dinner and since no one was allowed into the ICU ward at night, they would all go out to dinner together. While they ate they would then determine where the out-of-towners would stay that night.

Stephen suggested a restaurant that has a sufficient seating area for the whole family. Before they departed, Stephen left his cell phone number at the nurse's station, asking that if there were any changes, he reemphasized *any changes*, in his mother's condition, he'd appreciate a call.

During dinner, when the family discussed sleeping arrangements, Wanda advised that her travel agent had already made a reservation for her at one of the better motels in town.

Sandy's eyes met Trisha's across the table and each knew what each other was thinking - *our home is not good enough for her.*

It was two in the morning, and the critical care nurse was making a visual scan of all their sleeping patients through the long window. She noticed some movement from Velma Pearce and then her monitor began to sound. She put down the paperwork she had in her hand and quickly went into the ward. Reaching Velma's bedside, she saw that her patient's eyes were open and her hands were crossed on her chest. Immediately the door opened and nurses with the crash-cart entered.

"What's goin' on?" asked a nurse.

"She just opened her eyes."

The head nurse leaned over Velma and said, "Mrs. Pearce, you've had an accident and you're in the hospital. Can you hear me?" She continued to speak to her in soothing tones.

She turned to another nurse and said, "Please call Stephen Pearce to let him know that his mother woke up." Within a few minutes Velma's eyes closed and her breathing slowed to a normal rhythm.

The call was made to Stephen. After he thanked the nurse for the update, he placed the phone back on its cradle and lay back on his pillow.

"Was that the hospital?" asked Marianne.

"Yes. Mother woke up."

"Are you going over there?"

"No. I'll give the other kids a heads-up and we'll go over there in the morning. I'll tell them to swing by here for breakfast, if that's okay with you."

"Sure, as long as you'll help," she said with a grin.

He gave her a quick kiss and then he phoned each of his siblings.

"Sweetheart, did you remember to call the substitute to say you'd be out maybe another day or so?"

"Yes, dear. Now, go to sleep. We only have a couple of hours before that alarm rings. Love ya."

"Me, too."

*Salt is good; but if the salt
have lost its saltness,
wherewith will ye season it?
Have salt in yourselves.
And have peace one
with another.*

Mark 9:50 KJV

Matthew Henry Concise Commentary on the whole Bible says about Mark 9:50:

"Those that have the salt of grace, must show they have a living principle of grace in their hearts, which works out corrupt dispositions in the soul that would offend God, or our own consciences."

Chapter 15

On the third floor surgery ward, James awoke very early that morning from a restless night's sleep. The whole side of his face throbbed along with an added headache from what he surmised was lack of caffeine. He loved his coffee and drank several cups each day - right up until he retired for the night.

When the nurse came in to take his vital signs, he kept his jaw tight and talked through the slit of his mouth, asking, "What time is it?"

"Pardon me?"

"I asked, what time is it?"

This time she understood him and checked her watch. "Six o'clock."

"Oh," he groaned.

"Mr. Pearce, you are scheduled for surgery at nine this morning. I'm sorry but you won't be getting any breakfast."

The nurse left and James closed his eyes, hoping to go back to sleep. But, could not. He lay there replaying again and again in his mind the landing at the airport the day before. *How stupid can one person be to not wear their seatbelt? Rocky did a great job of bringing that Cessna to a halt after the tire blew. Don't know if I could've done that good of a job.*

The nurse came in and handed him a pill and held the glass of water for him, stating that he could take only a sip.

Within a few minutes he was asleep, but woke in about an hour when he felt someone's warm lips on his forehead. He struggled to open his eyes.

He blinked several times and then saw his wife's face looking down at him. He tried to smile, but winced when pain shot through his cheek.

"Hi, sweetheart. Did you get some sleep last night?"

He just shook his head, 'no'.

"The nurse told me that your surgery is scheduled for nine. I know you'll be glad when that's over with."

He nodded. His eyes closed.

"I called your office and told Sheila about your surgery and that you probably wouldn't be back in there for a few days."

"Okay." His mouth stayed ajar and his head slumped to the side – he was asleep.

Wanda smiled and then left the room to ask some questions of the nurses. Not having any answers, the nurse suggested that Wanda talk with the surgeon and turned to pick up the phone to call his office.

Returning the receiver to its cradle, she said, "Mrs. Pearce, the doctor asked that you come to his office. He just finished an operation and is in his office completing some paperwork. He's on the main floor in room 106."

"Thank you."

Wanda exited the elevator on the first floor and walked along the corridor looking at the room numbers on the doors until she came to 106. She knocked.

"Come in."

"I'm Mrs. Pearce."

"Please come in and sit down."

"Doctor, I'm interested in what you plan to do to repair my husband's face."

"Mrs. Pearce, your husband has a fractured cheekbone. Let me show you on this illustration here on the wall what a normal cheekbone looks like." With his index finger he first pointed to the top of the cheekbone. "You will notice that the cheekbone forms part of the eye socket. It protects the eyeball and supports it from below. It is also linked over here to the side of the nose and over here to the upper part of the jaw. We aren't sure at this point if your husband's eye socket is damaged."

"How will you go about repairing the cheekbone?"

"Well, once your husband is asleep I'll make a small cut about an inch long through his hair at his temple and put the cheekbone back in the right place. If it doesn't stay in place on its own, I may have to hold it in place with small Titanium plates and screws."

"My husband travels a lot. Will he be setting off metal detectors at the airports?" she asked with a smile.

He smiled back. "No."

"Is there any danger with this kind of surgery?"

"Mrs. Pearce, there's always an element of risk in any kind of surgery, but with this type of surgery the risk is very, very low. If there's any bleeding in and around his eye socket, which is quite rare, this could cause a problem with the eyesight immediately following surgery. In that case, he would be closely monitored for the first few hours after his operation."

"Would those plates and screws be removed after a period of time?"

"No. Those items tend not to cause problems unless they become infected."

Wanda let out a sigh of relief. "It doesn't sound as bad as what I had conjured up in my mind." She put out her hand to shake his hand. "Thank you, doctor. I appreciate your time. You've put me at ease."

"Mr. Pearce is going to be just fine. After surgery, he'll be in recovery for a while and then he'll be back in his room after that. Will you be in the surgery waiting room?"

"Most of the time. My mother-in-law is also here in the hospital and I will be checking on her in the ICU ward at different intervals."

"When the surgery is over, I'll be happy to visit with you and give you an update on your husband's condition. If you will, let the nurse's station on the surgery ward know whenever you leave to go to the ICU ward."

"I'll do that. Thank you, again, doctor."

Wanda looked at her watch as she walked toward the elevator. She saw that she would only have a few more minutes with James before he would be wheeled off to surgery.

Wanda was sitting beside James' bed when Paul, Sonja, Stephen and Cassie walked into the room. James was asleep, but Cassie leaned over and whispered his name and he awoke.

"Hey, baby brother, we've come to invite you to a party," said Cassie.

"Very funny," replied James.

She turned to Wanda. "Did you sleep okay?"

"I was so tired when I went to bed that I don't remember anything else after my head hit the pillow. Where's Gordon?"

"He and Trisha stayed with Mother," said Paul. He looked at James, "Hey, brother, we thought you might need a good laugh before going under the anesthesia."

"I could really do without any humor this morning." He slightly grinned, and that caused a shooting pain to run through his jaw. He flinched at which the family members frowned upon seeing the painful expression on his face.

"When are you headed for the operating room?"

Wanda spoke up, "Nine."

Paul looked at his watch, and said, "Ah, you've still got a little time. It's only 8:50."

"How's your mother?" Wanda asked.

"She came to during the night, but so far she hasn't spoken. She appears not to recognize anyone. She just stares."

"Excuse me, folks. Mr. Pearce needs to go for a ride," said two orderlies, as they wheeled in a gurney.

Cassie and Sonja leaned over and kissed their brother, telling him that they loved him. Paul and Stephen took turns telling him goodbye and that they, too, loved him.

"We'll be praying for you, little brother," said Cassie.

The four siblings watched as their brother was wheeled from the room, Cassie had her arm around Wanda's shoulders. Having two family members in dire straits was hard for the entire family.

"Wanda, how about a cup of coffee in the cafeteria?" asked Cassie.

"I'd love it."

"Mind if I tag along?" asked Sonja.

"Not at all," replied Wanda.

Everyone headed for an elevator, with the men getting off on the second floor, while the trio of women rode on down to the main floor.

As they exited the elevator, Cassie heard her name called. She turned to see her husband, Bob, walking toward them.

"Hi, honey. You got here earlier than you thought you would."

"I know. The highway was almost empty. I wondered if you had put on your Facebook page that I would be on the road - so please beware." Everyone grinned.

Bob greeted his sisters-in-law and then asked, "Where are you headed?"

"To get some coffee."

"Good, I could stand a cup right now. I went through a drive-in for a cup of coffee, but didn't get a taste of it until I was down the road a little. It was the worst tasting coffee I've ever had. Bitter. Bitter. Bitter. Must've been sittin' there in the pot for hours."

"Yuk," retorted Sonja.

Both Cassie and Sonja were pleased that Bob had shown up when he did. The two had never found it easy to talk with Wanda. But, they knew she needed some company in order to pass the time away while awaiting news of James' operation. With Bob there, they could discuss a lot more subjects than just Wanda's whirlwind lifestyle.

As they walked toward the cafeteria, Sonja couldn't help but ask the Lord's forgiveness for her feelings about

Wanda. *I feel so uncomfortable around her, Lord. She's my brother's wife and I would really like to like her, but . . . it's so hard.* Even though she had just prayed she didn't feel any better about the situation.

At a table, the four sipped on their coffee and discussed James' surgery. Wanda shared what information that she had been given. They were all intrigued by what she had found out.

"I'm mostly concerned as to how good of a doctor this surgeon really is."

Sonja, having lived in Middleton all her life, said, "Wanda, this may not be a large hospital, but because of the scenic ocean retreat of Middleton, it has attracted some good doctors. Their pay may not be fabulous, but they love the laid-back lifestyle offered here."

"Wanda, tell us about your kids and grandkids," said Cassie, quickly changing the subject. Just as quickly as she had asked the question, she hastily added, "Oops, that's right your two are still single, aren't they?"

"They are, but you know how young people are. Relationships seem to be quite different today. Lori has a long-distance relationship with a fellow veterinarian in Africa. He's doing research there and I guess their relationship consists mostly of daily emails and talks by 'Skype' – of course about animals.

"As for Stewart, he has a girlfriend. She's from his law firm. I think she's a paralegal. They're living together in a new apartment building in downtown Atlanta, with a great view of the city."

Cassie and Sonja both knew better than to show any emotion about that bit of news.

"As for their careers, both are doing just great. Matthew followed in his father's footsteps to become a lawyer and is with a thriving well-known firm in Atlanta.

"Krystal is a veterinarian at the Bronx Zoo. She was at the top of her class in veterinarian school and did her internship at that zoo. They liked her work so well that they kept her on. She works in their laboratory and finds that work extremely interesting. They have some outstanding exhibits at that zoo, from all over the world."

Bob sat up, very interested in what she was saying, as he had a great love of animals. He and Cassie have two very loving Havanese dogs. Cassie often jokes with her husband at times, "You talk nicer to those dogs than you do to me."

"Did she ever say what kind of unusual animals she's worked with?" asked Bob.

"The zoo is quite famous for rare animals from other countries, which means Krystal has to do a lot of research – and that is right up her alley. She always has her nose in a book or the computer screen. Ah . . . let me see. She's treated a ring-tailed mongoose and ah . . . a red panda."

Sonja interrupted her, "A red panda? I thought pandas were black and white."

"There are both kinds. Krystal said that the red ones have the cutest faces. I believe she said they come from the area around the Himalayas. She's also had the experience of working with a huge Indian rhinoceros' and some Asian elephants. She loves her work. When we talk on the phone, you'd think we were talking about her children, as she goes on and on about those animals."

Her listeners smiled.

Bob interjected, "Think I took up the wrong line of work. I talked with a counselor in college about changing my degree to the veterinarian courses, but when I found out that they only accept a limited number of students into the program, and also that they had to attend more than four years of college, I quickly tossed out that idea for something a bit easier . . ."

"And what was that?" interrupted Wanda.

"Architecture"

"Easier?" questioned Sonja. "A lot of mathematics is needed for that."

"Yeah, but he loves figures," said Cassie.

"That's right – all kinds of figures," he replied with a grin, using his hands to outline a female hourglass figure.

Cassie elbowed him in his side.

"Ouch. That hurt."

"It was meant to." She smirked.

Wanda looked at her watch and said, "I'd better get up to the surgery waiting room. The doctor said he would come there to let me know how the surgery went. I'll see all of you later."

"Do you want some company?" asked Cassie.

"I'm not very good company when I'm uptight. But, thanks, anyway. I'll see you." She walked away.

"Not sure about that gal. One minute she's pleasant and the next minute she's 'Miss Uppity'," Sonja lamented.

"Yeah. But, she can be nice at times, agreed?" asked Cassie.

"Yeah."

"Hey, girls. Cut her some slack. Right now she's on edge, waiting to hear about her husband's surgery," commented Bob. "Besides that, you two were blessed to be brought up in a home where right attitudes were stressed. I've always been quite proud of Cassie for not letting her TV career cause her head to swell. She's also helped me in many ways to keep my life in the right perspective. Wanda grew up as an only child in a well-to-do family and that's all she knows."

"You're right, but James knows better. He grew up in a different atmosphere, and he's let all that go by the wayside," commented Sonja.

Cassie interjected, "Well, James has let this new life that he's made for himself get in the way of his Christian upbringing. But you and I married Christian men and that has a lot to say for itself. We had someone who kept us grounded."

Sonja looked down in shame and nodded her head in agreement with her older sister.

"We'd better get back up to the ICU ward," said Cassie.

Sonja agreed.

As they walked to the elevator, Bob pulled Cassie aside and suggested they go for a bite to eat away from the hospital before going back up to see her mother. He could tell that his wife needed to get away for a few minutes.

"I'd like that. Sonja, we'll be back in a little while. Please tell the others that we'll be gone for just a short time. I've got my cell phone in case you need to get in touch with me. Okay?"

"Okay." They parted.

Walking arm and arm to the car, Cassie looked up at her husband and said, "Thanks."

"For what?"

"For being such a good husband." They both smiled at each other as Bob opened the car door for his wife.

They settled on finding a restaurant that served chili. The cooler weather called for something like that.

At the diner, they sat across from each other at the table. Bob asked, "Cassie, did James always have a bleak outlook on life? He seems to be so touchy."

"No. In fact, he was the life of the party at home. Many times, Daddy had to put a stop to his antics at the dinner table. There was more than once that he sent James to his room because he couldn't stop laughing over a joke that he had told.

"When James was born, I became a surrogate mother to him on occasions, as I was the oldest girl in the family. I loved putting him in my doll buggy and wheeling him around our yard. I had made him my baby.

"When he had some kind of problem growing up, he would come up to my room, knock on the door and ask to come in. He would get up on my bed and then with big sad eyes say, 'Cassie, I've got a problem.' Those eyes could melt me and break my heart. When I went away to college, he was the one I missed the most.

"Later, while in high school, he was the leader of our young group at church, elected by the youth at least three times in a row. He was not only a leader, but he loved life, which was quite contagious.

"Then he went away to college where he joined a fraternity, becoming a big-shot on campus. From that point on, he was never the James that I grew up with. Becoming a lawyer changed him even more.

"Honey, do you remember when James and Wanda came home for Daddy's funeral? It was as though he was a distant cousin who we hardly knew. He seemed pompous and detached from the family. They didn't stay long. They were in an all-fired hurry to get back to Portland for some big fancy-shamsy ball they just *had* to attend. They made everyone uncomfortable that day.

"I would sure like to see my baby brother back, again – as he once was."

Bob reached across the table to pat the back of her hand. "Someday, sweetheart. Hopefully, someday."

Chapter 16

The phone in the ICU waiting room had rung several times. Most of the calls were for the Pearce family from individuals who had read in the newspaper about Velma's accident and they were calling out of concern.

One of those many calls was from Pastor Simpson. He was overjoyed when he heard that Velma had become conscious. "How is she?" he asked.

Gordon answered, "Pastor, she's not responsive. She just stares off into space, which is very disconcerting. The doctor hasn't been in as yet this morning, so we haven't gotten a full report of her condition. We also hope to hear as to when they will operate on her hip."

"Gordon, how's James?"

"His eye began to bleed so they've had to work on that situation. But, they tell us it is rare, but not unusual for that to happen with the kind of surgery he had."

"Gordon, please call me whenever you do hear something about your mother. I have to preach a funeral this afternoon, so I won't be over to the hospital until later. I am still very concerned about her."

"Pastor, if you'll give me your phone number, I'll call and if you aren't at home, I'll leave a message for you."

The pastor chuckled. "Oh, Gordon, I, too, ride the technological wave just like you. I do have a cell phone, which I'm using right now. I'll give you that number."

"Thanks. I apologize if I offended you."

"Dear boy, you did not. Please give my love to the family. I'll talk with you later." He gave Gordon his home and cell phone numbers and then they said their goodbyes.

Pastor Simpson pushed the 'off' button on his cell phone and laid it down on the passenger seat beside him. He was sitting in his car in the driveway of the parsonage, ready to go visit a sick parishioner at their home prior to the funeral. *My dear Lord, she's opened her eyes, but now I pray thee, please open her mind. Much thanks, In Jesus' name I pray this. Amen.*

That afternoon, after the funeral, Pastor Simpson was kept busy updating Velma's condition to the many people who knew her. She was the topic of conversation with those who later attended the meal served to the family of the deceased.

I don't think Velma realizes just how much she is loved thought the pastor as he stood in the buffet line. *How many people take the time out of their busy schedules to care for others like Velma Pearce does? She's one in-a-million.*

His thoughts were interrupted by the lady standing behind him. "Pastor, try some of that potato salad over there. I made it and even if I may say so myself, it's very good."

"Thank you, Miss Templeton. I'll try some."

He felt someone poke his elbow. It was Mrs. Templeton, again. "Pastor, that red-velvet cake over there on the dessert table is also one that I made."

"Thank you. I'll get me a slice." *And you wonder why, Peter, that you have a larger waistline today than you did forty years ago. If you wouldn't try to please all the cooks in your congregation, you'd still have a size thirty-eight waist.* He chuckled to himself.

Another phone call that came to the waiting room was from Catherine Williams. She, too, was initially pleased to hear that Mrs. Pearce had awakened, but was again concerned when she heard that she was not responding vocally.

"We won't bring Samantha over there until she is more responsive. In the meantime, our family will continue to pray for Mrs. Pearce."

When Catherine hung up the phone she smiled when she recognized how good it felt to say 'We're praying.' She knew in her heart that she and her husband had finally gotten back on track with God.

Pastor Simpson had not received any calls from Velma's family at the hospital, which meant there was no change in her condition. He decided to drive over there, anyway.

Approaching the hospital elevator, he decided not to go to the waiting room, but go directly to Velma's room. He so wanted to see her with her eyes opened. He entered the ward and saw Stephen and Marianne sitting on each side of the bed.

Stephen rose from his chair to greet the dear gentleman who had been such a part of his life for so many years. "Pastor, nice to see you."

"Stephen. Marianne." He walked to the foot of the bed. "How is she?"

"No change. She just stares straight ahead and turns her head ever so slightly from time to time."

Stephen backed his chair away from the bed so that the pastor could stand at Velma's side.

"Velma. This is Pastor Simpson." He had leaned way over toward her face.

As he began to speak to her, Stephen motioned to Marianne with his head in the direction of the door, and she got up and followed him out of the room.

Pastor Simpson took a hold of Velma's hand, gently rubbing the back of it. "Velma. Dear Velma, I wish I knew if you can hear me. We've never had a problem talking with each other, so I want to be very open with you."

Velma stared straight up, with no indication that she heard him.

He looked around and saw that he was alone with Velma. "Mrs. Johnson went home to be with the Lord the other day and we held her funeral today. Velma, do you know how many people at the funeral asked about you? You are so precious in the hearts of so many people – young and old.

"It's been a year now since my beloved Eva went home to be with the Lord. I know she wouldn't mind if I said to you, Velma, you are a precious lady to others and . . . to me. Um . . . and I guess I might as well be truthful with you, Velma, by telling you that I have come to recognize that I have more feelings for you than just as your pastor or friend. Does that surprise you?" When her countenance did not change, he groaned and sighed deeply in his spirit.

He again looked around, hoping no one was near enough to have heard what he had just said. He was not ashamed, but it was too personal. Then he waited for a moment or two before continuing with his discourse. Instead, he changed it into a silent prayer. *Oh Lord, I do wish she could hear me. I feel so useless. How can I console her family when at this moment I'm so disturbed in my own spirit about her? What can I say to them to encourage them to hold on until You perform a miracle in their mother's life? Help me, Lord.*

He continued to stand at her side; his eyes were closed and his heart was in a prayerful state. He was interrupted when Gordon and Trisha entered the room.

"Pastor Simpson. Stephen told us that you were in here visiting with Mother."

He greeted them and then said, "I'm like all of you, though, I would sure like it if she answered me back."

"I know what you mean. It's difficult for all of us to see her in this state of limbo."

"How's James?"

"He's recovering nicely. The doctor said he felt the surgery went well and that he should have a good recovery. He's in his own room now and I think Wanda is there with him, along with Paul and Sandy."

"You're family has had their hands full with two members hospitalized here."

"Pastor, it's been surreal."

"If you'll excuse me, I think I'll go up and see James."

"Sure." Gordon extended his hand and said, "Pastor, you don't know how much we appreciate your presence here with us. We're grateful for how much you care about our family."

"It's been my pleasure for years to know the Pearce family." He turned to go, "I'll talk with you later, Gordon. Goodbye, Trisha."

After visiting with James, Pastor Peter Simpson started for home, almost in a daze. So much had happened over the past couple of weeks. Unbeknownst to his congregation, he had sent word to the district office of his desire to resign his pastorate.

He had not come to that decision instantaneously, but it was one that he had prayerfully considered for some time. He knew that he was too old now to continue with the rigorous schedule that was set before him each day. He had a good secretary who kept him on track, but still he tired of the constant demand for his time.

In a month he would give his last sermon at his church. And now on top of that weighty situation, Velma is in critical condition. *How much more can I take. This eighty-year-old is going to need a whole lot of Your Grace in the next few weeks, Lord. I sure can't handle all of this on my own. I learned a long time ago, that You are in control – not me.*

He decided to drive down to the waterfront where he could get out and walk along the deserted beach. With his hands in his overcoat pocket to keep them warm, he sauntered ever so slowly down the beach, listening to the waves as they lapped at the shoreline. He had always found that the huge expanse of the Pacific Ocean gave him a sense of peace.

His eyes caught sight of a huge container ship way off in the distance. As he watched it sailing north, he thought, *probably headed for Seattle.* As he walked, he thought *life is like that ship sailing on the open sea. The captain steers it out to sea, headed for a certain destination, but at the same time uncertain as to difficult waters that he may encounter.*

I heard Captain Sullivan once say, 'When in a storm, my ship rides on the waves that catapult it upward and then plunges it downward only to catch the next wave that sends it high again to the pinnacle of that wave. I can only believe that my past experiences in handling any such situation would be enough now to see me through.'

His thoughts continued. *You know, Peter, that's just like us. As we head in a certain direction, suddenly we encounter the ups and downs of life's situations. We can't help but wonder if we'll lose our ability to trust God in this situation and surely falter as we believe only in ourselves. Or . . . will we steadily move on with God as our Captain.*

With all those thoughts running through his head he felt like a ship adrift at sea. Ever since Eva's death, he had kept working, working as intense as he could and leaving no time to give in to despondency. He knew that would only consume him.

Now with his retirement approaching and the new revelation of his feelings toward Velma, he stood looking out to sea, thoroughly bewildered as to his future.

Lord, I'm a pastor of the Gospel that teaches us not to give in to feelings. I have to admit, Lord, I feel like a ship that has broken down and is floundering out at sea. Help me, Lord.

His eyes again scanned the horizon and he was quite surprised to see just how far that container ship had now sailed from when he saw it last. He smiled as he realized, *it just keeps on sailing. I guess that's what you want me to do, Lord. You said that You would direct my steps, and that's exactly what I'm gonna let You do.* He threw back his shoulders and said aloud, "I just need to keep on keeping on."

Peter Simpson turned and walked with a slow gait back to his car. The heaviness which had enveloped him for so many months had now lifted in just that short period of time.

The tide had earlier receded, which left the sand wet. There, very prominently in the sand, he recognized his own recent footprints from when he had walked in the other direction. He smiled and said, "Just keep right on walking, Peter. The Lord is directing your footsteps."

Chapter 17

Velma's doctor came through the door of the ward on his evening rounds and made his way from one patient to another. Sonja and Jeff were at Velma's bedside when he arrived at her bed.

Jeff stood to acknowledge the doctor, while Sonja just turned in her chair to greet him.

"Well, folks, it looks like we'll take your mother to surgery in the morning to fix that hip. It's a good thing she has been immobile since the accident. We hope that no more damage has been done to her hip over the past couple of days."

"When is the surgery?" asked Sonja.

"She's on the schedule for the first surgery at 8 a.m. She'll probably be in recovery for several hours. Then she'll be placed on the surgery ward."

"What about the attack she had? Was it a stroke or mild-heart attack as thought?" questioned Sonja.

"All the tests have shown no damage to her heart, and she's had no more episodes, so the cardiologist and I can only speculate that her brain was trying to regain consciousness and that produced that spasmodic reaction in her body."

"Oh," said Sonja, as she leaned against the back of the chair and allowed a huge sigh to escape. "That's good news."

"Yes, it is. We would not have proceeded with the surgery had there been any doubt in our mind." He turned to leave and then turned back, "The family can wait in the surgery waiting room on the third floor tomorrow. I'll come there to update you on the results of the surgery."

"Thank you, doctor." Sonja stood up and extended her hand to him. "We're grateful for all that you've done for our mother."

"My pleasure."

Sonja waited a moment and then went to the waiting room to inform her siblings about the surgery in the morning.

Early the next morning, all five of the Pearce children and their spouses were on hand for the surgery, except for Wanda. She was in James' room, reassuring him that his mother would be all right. He would be released later in the morning, depending on whether the bleeding in his eye had stopped. The two would then join the others during their wait for the completion of their mother's surgery.

The orthopedic surgeon stopped by the ICU waiting room on his way to scrub for the surgery. He wanted to reassure them that he would do all that he could do to make their mother's surgery a success story.

"Doctor, what does this type of surgery entail?" asked Cassie.

"I'll try to explain it to you in layman's terms. She has a fractured right hip, but also there is osteoarthritis in that hip. The wear and tear of aging causes the cartilage covering the joint surfaces to wear out. We'll first make a ten-to-twelve inch incision on the side of the hip. We'll remove the head of the thighbone or what it's also called - the femur."

Trisha let out a sharp squeal and then held her hand tightly over her mouth. The doctor stopped talking as everyone had turned to look at Trisha.

Gordon patted her leg, "You okay, honey?"

Trisha just nodded her head rapidly, but her scrunched-up eyes that were looking at everyone from over her hand, belied her.

"She's got a weak constitution," said her husband, as he put his arm around his wife's shoulders.

The surgeon smiled and then continued on, "The muscles are split or detached from the hip, allowing the hip to be dislocated. We will then replace the upper end of the thighbone that constitutes the ball-and-socket mechanism of the hip with artificial implants. We'll also replace the damaged cartilage with new joint material."

Gordon felt his wife's shoulders compress as the doctor spoke. He leaned over and kissed her cheek.

"Will she be asleep?" asked Sonja.

"In your mother's case, since she was unconscious for a time and due to her age, we prefer not to place her under general anesthesia, but we'll use regional anesthesia. That means she will *not* feel the area of the surgery and she'll be sleepy, but will be awake during the surgery."

"Are you sure she won't feel what's going on?" asked Marianne.

"I'm sure. Also, during the surgery we will use a compression pump which will squeeze her leg to keep the blood circulating to help prevent blood clots."

"You said 'help to prevent,' is there any chance she may get a blood clot?"

"Ma'am, that is one question that is impossible to answer. I can promise you that should that occur, we will keep a close watch on her in recovery and we'll take steps to dissolve the clot. Is there anything else you might be concerned about?"

"What kind of recovery time are we looking at?" asked Stephen.

"Most people go home within a few days to a week after surgery. Should she need more extensive rehab or if she doesn't have someone who can help at home, she would then need to go to a specialized rehab center for more treatment."

"Oh, she'll have plenty of help," said Gordon. "We'll see to that."

"Good."

"Doctor, what about right after the surgery? How long will she be in recovery?" asked Paul.

"Not too long, since she won't be put to sleep before surgery. Once again, let me reassure you I'll be back in here as soon as the surgery is over to give you a complete update on her condition. In the meantime, folks, may I suggest you relax and enjoy your time together. My surgery team has your mother's best interest at heart. We've all been through this type of surgery multiple times and we pride ourselves on giving the patient the utmost opportunity for a new lease on life." He smiled, waved his hand in a goodbye gesture and left the room.

Sonja walked over to the coffee urn to sniff for the freshness of the coffee in the pot. "We're set for the next little while - this coffee is fresh."

"I'm walking down the hall to James' room and let 'em know what the doctor told us," said Cassie.

"I'll go with you," said Bill.

"Me, too," added Gordon. He motioned for his wife, Trisha, to come with him.

The phone in the waiting room rang. A visitor sitting near the phone picked it up. "Waiting room . . . ah . . . let me ask. Is there a Stephen Pearson here?"

"I would wager that call is for me. I'm Stephen Pearce" He took the receiver, "Hello, this is Stephen Pearce."

It was Catherine Williams calling to ask about Velma's condition. Stephen told her that she would soon be on her way to the operating room to get a new hip and that she could call back later to find out the results.

Stephen had no sooner placed the receiver on the cradle, when it rang again. He answered it and it was Pastor Simpson. Gordon had already texted him regarding his mother's surgery to take place this morning, but he did not reply back. He was now calling to let the family know that he was on his way over there.

Within a few minutes, Mrs. Ramirez phoned to ask about Mrs. Pearce. She was informed of the surgery about to take place and that Velma would be in recovery for quite some time. "Mrs. Ramirez, I should tell you that my mother became conscious yesterday, but is still not responding at all. It's up to you, but I believe it would be just fine if the two of you would like to come and visit her tomorrow. She'll be in her own room by then."

Mrs. Ramirez was pleased with the outcome of the conversation. Before she left for work, she wrote a note regarding Mrs. Pearce and left it on the table for Tony to see when he got home from school.

She was quite aware that her son was still having problems coping with his part in Mrs. Pearce's hospitalization. She knew that if he could see her conscious, that he might be able to handle the situation better.

The Pearce family walked to the entrance of the ICU ward to await their mother being wheeled out on her way to the operating room.

Over at the police precinct, the desk sergeant strolled over to Sgt. Jackson's desk. "Hey, Jackson, I saw in the newspaper the article about the old lady who got hit by that kid's bike. What's happenin' with that case? I haven't seen any paperwork come through."

"Nothin's happening at the moment. I checked with the nurse's station this morning and was told that the lady would be having surgery today. The good news is that she is no longer unconscious. But . . . the bad news is that she is unresponsive. Until we get her side of the story, the whole matter will just have to sit."

"Who's gonna be responsible for the medical bills?"

"That'll be another huge problem for her. The kid's mom works at a convenience store and has no insurance. The lady's medical insurance company will probably reject any claims for the incident since the person hitting her is deemed responsible."

"Wow. The medical bills are probably piling up."

"You can say that again. I plan to take Tony over to the hospital again in a couple of days. Poor kid, he's taking this whole thing pretty hard."

"You're taking this thing pretty personal yourself, fella."

"Maybe so." With a huge sigh, he continued, "Winston, when you've had a child of your own die like I have, ya watch out for other kids to make sure they get every opportunity to live. I mean, really live a good life. As you know, my son was killed in a swimming accident when he dove off a cliff into untested waters. By that, I mean that he and the kids he was with had no knowledge as to the depth of the water. You know how young preteens can be? They just want to have fun. He was challenged by the other kids to be first one off the cliff and he accepted their challenge."

The desk sergeant put his hand on Sgt. Jackson's shoulder. "I only heard parts of that story, but never the whole thing. I . . . um . . . always hesitated to ask you about it. That must've been rough for you and your wife."

"It was and as a matter of fact, still is for my wife even though it's been over twelve years. But, I made up my mind a couple of years ago to let it go. Now, I just try to think of the good times we had together like at Christmas, his birthday parties, baseball games and his first bike.

"My wife, on the other hand, hasn't completely dealt with her grief, but she's trying. She became a volunteer for the CASA program - putting her time to good use."

"CASA? Oh, yeah, I heard about that program. They sponsor young kids with problems, don't they?"

"Well, the kids aren't generally the problem, it's really the parents who are either druggies, alcoholics or are child abusers."

"I know you must be proud of Connie's work with those kids."

"I am. You know, Winston, yesterday when I saw Tony's bike lying there crumpled on the ground; my first thought was of my son's bike. He fell off the very first time he got on it. I had run behind him for about a quarter of a block with my hand on the back fender stabilizing him, and then I let go and let him pedal it by himself. He did fine for a few feet, but then the bike began to wobble and I knew he was about to take a spill.

"When it happened, I was scared spitless when I saw him lying there on the ground, but as I reached him, he looked up and said, "Did you see me, Dad. I rode it all by myself." He got up and looked at me with a big smile. His bike was the only thing scraped up. Boys - they seem to get pleasure from being daring."

"We were just as adventurous when we were that age. I've got girls, Jackson, and they are a whole different ballgame from boys." He smiled and Sgt. Jackson returned the smile.

"I know what you mean. We had one girl at the time our boy was alive, and then we had another one afterwards. She was one of those *accident* babies. You know . . . the kind you don't plan for. She's pretty special."

The desk sergeant's phone began to ring, so he went back to his desk to answer it.

Sgt. Jackson sat there in his chair, heavy with thought. Finally he thought *Yup, I need to get Tony over to that hospital in a couple of days.*

Sitting there, Sgt. Jackson recalled the conversation he had with his wife the night before. It had all started at dinner when he had mentioned Tony Ramirez in just a general conversation. Connie blew up, leaving the table to take her dish over to the sink. She continued to busy herself, ignoring Jack, as though he wasn't even in the room.

What did I say that set her off? He got up, picked up his plate and silverware to walk to the sink. He reached around his wife to place them in the sink. She stood ridged, neither one said a word.

He walked out the back door and sat on the porch steps. *Why does she get so upset when I talk about Tony? Can't she see that dealing with him is a part of my work?* He let out a deep sigh and then shook his head in exasperation.

───────────

Chapter 18

The orderlies from the operating room wheeled the gurney into the ICU ward to take Velma to surgery. Her family members stood on either side of the doorway, each one with their thoughts, surging through their mind. *If only she could speak,* was the only thought going through Cassie's mind.

Wanda had scooted downstairs from her husband's bedside to be with the family at this precarious time in the lives of the Pearce family. James had asked her to be there to stand in for him.

As the double doors opened, in an almost choreographed scene, the Pearce children and grandchildren grabbed the hand of the one standing next to them. Some held their breath while others gasped to see their eighty-year-old mother on that gurney - motionless.

Stephen held out his hand to stop the orderlies and asked, "Could we have a moment with her?"

Each family member bent over to kiss their mother or grandmother and whispered their own thoughts to her. Tears were in the eyes of some, while others were stiff in their mannerisms, which was the only way they knew how to handle this very difficult time. Some had doubts as to the outcome of the surgery, while others were confident that God would be in charge of the situation, and bring their mother through with flying colors.

They watched as the gurney was rolled down the hall. Cassie and Sonja, in a sudden decision, broke out of the pack and ran up to walk alongside of their mother until they reached the operating room's double doors.

The doors closed, leaving the two sisters standing there, immobile, almost like waxed figures. Then Cassie put her arms around her younger sister and said, "She'll be all right, Sonja. We now must be positive in our thinking."

"I know. I guess it's upsetting for me to see Mother so helpless. She's always been the strong one in the family, seeing that we were all taken care of. Cassie, what if we lose her?"

"Sonja, that's enough of that kind of talk. Come on; let's go to the waiting room with the others."

Connie Jackson walked into the beauty shop for her nine-thirty appointment. For the past five years she had this standing appointment once a week to get a shampoo and set. She was doing this and everything else in her power to regain the vanished joy that had left her when their son died.

Twice a week she spends two hours in a water-aerobics class at a local gym. She had found that those two hours relax her more than anything else.

She came to recognize that the one thing that helped the most to cope with life was her time with other young people when she volunteered with the guardian ad litem program. Witnessing the good that came from her time being an advocate for young boys and girls made her feel worthwhile.

She had slept very little the night before, tossing and turning. Her mind had been on Mrs. Pearce, the gracious lady who had become very important to her. *How could anyone be so supportive of that boy who hurt Velma Pearce? I know that in my line of work I have to stand up for kids almost every day. But, not this time. That boy had to have seen Velma standing there.* She turned onto her back. *She's a Christian, so where was God in all of this? This whole thing has me so frustrated.* She rolled to her side and looked at her husband, who was sound asleep. *Tony! Tony! Tony! That's all he talks about for the past couple of days.* She took in a long breath of air, closed her eyes and let it out slowly. *He can be so exasperating at times.*

Now, as she walked into the beauty shop, she noticed that the place seemed empty. She and one other lady, already in the midst of a haircut, were the only ones to occupy customer chairs. She spotted two other hairdressers; one was sweeping, while the other was filing her fingernails.

"Mornin', ladies," said Connie. Those in the room acknowledged her greeting.

Her beautician's chair was positioned next to the lady getting the haircut, so soon after having her hair washed; a lot of conversation took place between the four ladies. Mostly, the topics were in general nature, but then . . .

"Did you hear about the old lady who got mowed down by that kid's bicycle?" asked the customer. "The newspaper said this morning that the kid has not been charged. How come, I ask?" questioned the customer.

"Don't know. He's probably the son of someone who's well acquainted with the mayor or one of the councilmen. You know how that goes. It's who you know in this town," remarked Connie's young beautician.

"Well, the old lady's time was probably up, and that's her way of meeting her maker," said the customer, smugly.

Connie clenched her lips together as she would not respond to such nonsense. Nevertheless, her mind went rapidly to thoughts of Velma passing away. *She can't die. She's the one person who seems to understand the heartache I've experienced. She lost a baby at birth.* Those all-encompassing thoughts had kept her from hearing any more of what the others were saying.

Connie was so pleased when the customer's cape was removed by the beautician; she'd be leaving. *Thankfully, she'll be gone in a couple of minutes and I won't have to hear any more of their garbage.*

"Ms. Jackson," said Connie's hairdresser, backing away from her with her scissors pointed skyward. "Your husband's a police officer, right? What does he say about that accident and was it really an accident?"

"Ah . . . my husband doesn't bring his work home. He's good about leaving it at the police station."

"So, he's had no opinion about the situation?"

"If he has, he's not shared it with me." Connie knew that was not the whole truth, but she also was aware that it was unfair to her husband to divulge any of his police business.

When her appointment was finished, Connie walked to her car, opened the door and got in. She sat there for a few moments, her hands on the steering wheel. *This whole situation with Velma has caused a rift in my relationship with Jack. We don't need that. I guess I've been too hasty to place blame. I need to wait for all the facts to come in before I make a judgment.* She was surprised at her change of heart, but realized that the conversation in the beauty parlor had made her stop and re-evaluate the situation.

Connie started for home, but waiting in the inside lane at a stop light, she abruptly looked in her right-side mirror and saw no vehicle coming up on her right. Then making a quick glance to her right over her shoulder to double check, she made the right-hand turn from that inside lane. *If I get stopped for making an illegal turn, the headlines on this evening's newspaper will read, 'Police officer's wife arrested for illegal maneuver.'* She grinned.

"Whew! I made it." With no sound of a police car's siren behind her, she headed toward Starbucks. *I need to get Jack a latté – and take it to him.* She smiled as she pulled into the drive-thru lane at the coffee shop. *I hope he's at the precinct.*

She pulled her car into the police station parking lot and noticed Jack's police vehicle was parked there. She parked, got out and walked only a few steps when she realized that she had left the latté in the cup holder in the car. She grinned at her 'CRS' (Can't Remember Syndrome), and walked back to the car to fetch the 'I'm sorry' token.

Heads turned as Connie came through the front door. She was a very pretty woman, holding nicely to the looks of a thirty-year-old, while actually being forty-five. She noticed that the precinct was quiet, with no perpetrators being questioned; only police officers, staring down at paperwork on their desk or on the phone.

Connie walked back toward Jack's desk with the Starbuck's coffee cup in her hand. His co-workers began making loud comments, as only men can do when they see a spouse doing something nice for her husband.

"You're just jealous," she joked as she passed by each desk.

Jack smiled as she drew near him. The deadly silence that prevailed at breakfast was now put to rest.

"I'm sorry, sweetheart. I was wrong." she said softly as she neared him. Her eyes sparkled as she handed him his treat.

Chapter 19

James was released from the hospital but would need to return to the doctor's office in three days. He had now joined his family in the waiting room, and the topic of conversation for the first few minutes was about his swollen and badly bruised face. He was not as tightlipped as before the surgery, but he still spoke through his teeth, keeping his jaws as immobile as possible.

It was not unusual to see one or more members of the family to check the time. Their patience after two days of waiting was now wearing quite thin.

"Does anyone know anything about this kid's family?" asked James.

"Not much," replied Stephen.

"Since he's culpable for the accident, we need to make sure his family can pay for Mom's medical bills," said James, the lawyer aspect in him rising to the forefront.

"James, that won't happen," responded Stephen.

"Whatta ya mean?"

"Tony's mother is a single mother who works at a convenience store and doesn't have any insurance. She's a hard-working Mexican lady – who has her citizenship . . . and . . . her husband left her years ago."

James shuddered when he heard it was a Mexican woman. He'd had a bad taste in his mouth for Mexicans, having dealt with a few unscrupulous ones in the Portland area. "We'll find a way around that. "

"How," asked Sonja.

"Sue."

"Sue?" came forth in unison from the family members.

"What's the old saying – you can't get blood out of a turnip," said Gordon.

"Don't worry Gordon, I'll find a way." The wheels of justice began to whirl in James' head. He thought *you don't know me. My mother is **not** going to be the brunt of this accident.*

Cassie sat looking at her younger brother, aghast at what he might be planning to do. Heartbroken, she thought *I don't know him anymore.* She noticed that his demeanor was like that of a tenacious bulldog and his eyes piercing like that of a jaguar as it waits to pounce on its prey.

Cassie had become quite good at recognizing certain personality traits after years of interviewing people on the set of her television show. To the amazement of her co-anchor she had an uncanny ability to read a person not only from their demeanor, but also their body language, the eyes and even the forehead. Once, she told a friend, 'If you have straight lines across your forehead that tells me that you are a workaholic. If there are half-circles above your eyes, it means you're a 'people' person. If small vertical lines form between their eyes, especially deep ones, which means you are dogmatic in nature, then I need to be careful of how I ask them a question.'

James looked at his wife and demanded, "Gimme my cell phone."

Wanda fished around in her purse and pulled out his phone that she had kept during his surgery. James grabbed the phone from her hand and quickly scanned downward and then pressed a number and waited for an answer.

"Greg, James here. Yeah . . . yeah . . . I'm okay. It's just a small setback. I know . . . sorry, but I have to talk through my teeth for a while. Say, can you handle everything there for a few days? I'm going to be needed here to make sure that my mother's legal matters are taken care of, properly.

"Do me a favor? Run a check on . . . hold on just a minute. Stephen, what's the boy's mother's name?"

"Ah . . . oh, um, Consuela Ramirez," replied Stephen, quite reluctantly.

"Greg, find anything you can on a Consuela Ramirez. She has a son named Anthony or Tony for short. Yeah . . . uh-huh . . . Okay . . .

"And Greg, her old man ran out on her some time ago. She thinks he's in Mexico. Hold on . . .

"Stephen, what's the kid's dad's name?"

"I have no idea," said Stephen – his patience was beginning to run thin.

"You may have to tap into your sources in Mexico to find him. Call me when you find out anything." James pressed the 'off' button and put his phone in his jacket pocket. "No problem, family. We'll get to the bottom of this."

A deep silence filled the room.

"James, what good is that going to do?" Sonja broke the silence.

"That woman may have family with money. The only way we'll know is if we check her out.

Salt in an Unsavory World

"If anyone can find her family, Greg can. He's been with our firm for ten years, after relocating from a big firm in Chicago. One time, there in Chicago, he was retained to defend a big mobster for murder. Greg needed to find the one man who could testify that the mob boss was with him in Miami at the time of the murder. That person had been in hiding for the past year. Greg and a couple of other fellas finally tracked him down – in Italy. I often tease him that he should have been a detective instead of a lawyer."

The room was still very quiet, the family stunned by James' appalling attitude. He had not bothered to discuss the matter with the rest of the family before taking the situation into his own hands.

Paul was about to say something when the orthopedic surgeon walked through the door. Everyone rose to meet him, anxious to hear what he had to say.

"You'll be glad to know that your mother is in recovery and she's doing just fine. The hip replacement went well. I'm very pleased with the way it turned out. She'll probably be in recovery for about three to four hours. After that she'll be taken to a room here on the surgery floor. You can ask at the nurse's station which room she'll be in."

≈

The Pearce family decided to leave the hospital for some fresh air, exercise and a good hamburger and fries at a restaurant that had been a family favorite for years. Cassie and Bob said they would stay behind and continue to wait since they had gone out earlier.

Before leaving the waiting room, James said, "Sure hope they have something I can eat or drink. There's no way I can chew on a hamburger. But, I'll go anyway."

Soon after the room emptied of the family, Bob reach over and took a hold of Cassie's hand. "You're awful quiet."

"Bob, I'm so disappointed in this turn of events."

"You mean with James taking control?"

"Yes. I might have agreed with him if only he had talked it over with the family first. But to bull-doggedly take charge was unconscionable."

"You're right, but now that it's been done, we have to wait and see what his next move is going to be whenever he receives any information about the Ramirez family. In the meantime, we'll just have to believe that God will intervene in the situation before it gets out of hand."

Cassie nodded her head in agreement.

At lunch, the family was fairly quiet, as they were still digesting what had transpired in the waiting room with James.

The mood was lifted when in through the front door came Cheri, the daughter of Sonja and Jeff, and Lori, the daughter of Gordon and Trisha.

"Mom called me to join the family on my lunch hour and then I called Lori. And . . . here we are," chirped Cheri.

"You girls are gorgeous," said Sandy. "I love your auburn hair. Girls, I can't believe I haven't seen you for over four or five years.

"I wasn't able to make the trip with Paul when he came for your grandmother's seventy-fifth birthday party. I was still in the hospital after my gall-bladder surgery."

"It has been a long time," said Cheri, her hair in a short, cropped style that framed her face.

Lori remarked, "Thanks for the compliment, Aunt Sandy. But, you know what, having this color of hair isn't always enjoyable. I can't wear some colors because they clash with my hair. But, the older I get the more I like it. I hated it in elementary school when I got teased about my freckles and my red hair. Now, I'm grateful that Grandpa passed his hair color on to Aunt Cassie and also to us grandchildren." Lori's hair is long and shiny and resembles a model's hair in the shampoo ads on television.

"Come and sit down, girls," said Jeff.

"Mom, how's Grandma?" asked Cheri, the older of the two girls.

"She's out of surgery and in recovery right now. Your Aunt Cassie and Uncle Bob would have been here with us but decided to stay behind in the waiting room.

Wanda sat observing the family members as they chatted with one another, awaiting their food. *They aren't too friendly to James. I guess it must be that they know he has a hard time talking.*

How wrong she was. It had not been an hour since James made the call to his co-worker, and right now the family was still having a hard time accepting the audacious move he had made to exercise *his* authority for the whole Pearce family.

Sonja was thankful that Cheri had shown up, as she and Lori would keep conversation lively with anecdotes about the children they teach. Cheri is a fifth-grade teacher, while Lori teaches kindergarten.

Wanda and James, on the other-hand were not enjoying this family gathering, unable to appreciate small-town talk.

At times they looked at each other, and one or the other would roll their eyes as if to say, 'boring'!

Cheri was sitting next to her Uncle Paul and quite interested in his line of work as her own husband was a parole officer for Grays Harbor County. "Uncle Paul, are you still enjoying your job there at the prison?"

"I sure am, Cheri. I've enjoyed it even more since I don't have to be down with the prisoners in their cages. My work now is with individual inmates, counseling them as to what is possible for them on the outside when they are released. My goal is to see how many of those men will never again set foot in a prison."

Their conversation had drawn the attention of the others at the table, but was halted for a couple of minutes while the food was being served by the waitress.

"What techniques are the most beneficial in reaching these men?" asked Gordon.

"I wouldn't know if you want it a technique, but I try to reach a man for who he is. What were his interests growing up, and especially which ones were unfulfilled. One of the best programs that our prison warden has allowed into the system is our faith-based ministry. It has been a real success in rehabilitating men."

"How so?" asked Jeff.

"We have dormitories set up for those who seem to honestly desire to better themselves by living in a separate area where they can attend Bible classes and chapel."

"That's interesting. I've never heard of such a program," commented Gordon.

"I have to tell you, there have been great success stories that come from men who have been in the program and are paroled now. Of course, there are also those men who asked to be put in the faith-based dorms just so that they didn't have to put up with possible danger from some inmate that they had confrontation with earlier."

"Do you mean, Uncle Paul that those men in the program have to study the Bible?" asked Cheri.

"Yes. They have classes using administrative-approved Christian material and they are tested on it. They also can have time to attend chapel services, ask questions of the chaplain, or just get advice. Don't misunderstand me, they don't have a life of luxury, they, too, have to work in assigned jobs along with the general population."

"I've never heard that before, but I'm pleased to know that it takes place. If those men find out that a relationship with the Lord can change their lives, it will surely make a difference in their outlook on life," Gordon remarked. "Make a real change," he added.

James sat there sickened by this talk of religion. *Leave it alone, folks. I don't want to hear it. Just let me out of here.* He busied himself pressing the potatoes in the potato soup against the side of the bowl so that it would slide down easier. He couldn't wait until the meal was over and they could go back to the hospital. It had been over an hour since he'd made the call to Greg when his wish to get out of there was realized. His cell phone rang.

I'm saved by the bell thought James. He excused himself from the table to answer the call - outside. The family members looked at one another, wondering if it was the call from his co-worker with news about the Ramirez family. They watched through the big window as James paced back and forth on the sidewalk like that of a caged animal. He made gestures in the air with his hands and at times threw his fist in the air with a look on his face that showed great ire.

When he walked back inside, his demeanor showed of great frustration. He sat down and without a word picked up his spoon to finish his soup. But, suddenly his left hand went to the side of his face and he grimaced from the pain. All that shouting to his co-worker had probably caused the onslaught.

"Bad news?" asked Stephen.

"Could say that," James replied, without even looking up from his bowl of soup.

"What's the matter, darlin'?" queried Wanda.

"Oh . . . ah . . . Greg has a lot of connections around the U.S. and Mexico. He made some quick phone calls, but is having some problems with that corrupt, immoral Mexican government. They're withholding information about the Ramirez family. The irony of it all is that Greg usually gets what he's after. He should have pushed harder. Can't get over his disregard for how important this matter is to me."

There was silence from the other members of the family. But, they were all thinking in the same vein though, hoping that the search would be to no avail. James' words 'how important this matter is to me' reverberated in Stephen's mind.

James continued, "Incompetency! That's exactly what it is. I had to tell this man ways of getting around that tainted government. He'd better go ahead now with his usual brute-force tenacity to find that family or he'll have me to answer to." He paused . . . and then, "I'm gonna head back over to the hospital." He turned to his wife, and in a commanding tone, said, "Let's go."

She got up to follow him out of the restaurant. It was quite apparent to everyone at the table that even Wanda was also bewildered at her husband's attitude. James had been so preoccupied with his own thoughts that he walked right out without paying his portion of the bill.

Everyone was aghast at his insolent attitude - and his distasteful reference to Mexicans was something new to them all.

Sonja shook her head and said, "James. James. James. He has become so prideful. If Daddy were here right now, he would've said . . ."

Gordon interrupted her. "I know what you're referring to, Sis. Let me tell it. I remember it, word for word because he had said it to me while I was growing up." Gordon wagged his finger and also lowered his voice an octave - imitating his father. "'Son, you're prideful ways are going to get you into trouble. The Bible says *pride goeth before destruction, and a haughty spirit before a fall.*' Trouble? What kind of trouble? I couldn't comprehend at that age what sort of trouble a prideful spirit could bring."

The Pearce siblings laughed, remembering that they, too, had received that same dressing-down from their dad - many times. Cassie revealed her memories of run-ins with him on that subject and how she used that same Bible scripture with her kids - with the same non-effect, until they were older, that is.

"When I went on television, our oldest daughter reminded me of what Bob and I had said to her, growing up. Then she wagged her finger in my face - mimicking me

- and said, 'Mom, if you ever get the big-head about being on TV, I'll knock your block off.' She was twenty then, so I couldn't scold her for being insolent to her mother. But, between images of Sarah's and Dad's finger being waved in my face, I took to heart what they had said. Believe me when you have people expressing their admiration for you, it's easy to slip into pride. So that is something I have to constantly keep in check."

The family smiled.

Gordon picked back up the conversation from there, "What bothers me the most is that you'd have thought that James' arrogant attitude would have changed to some degree of gratefulness after experiencing that accident at the airport. I would hope if that had been me, I would've been so thankful to be alive that I would want to stop to smell the roses - more often."

> *"Let your speech be always with grace,*
>
> *seasoned with salt,*
>
> *that ye may know how*
>
> *ye ought to answer every man."*
>
> **Colossians 4:6** KJV

Chapter 20

"Pearce family," called out the nurse as her eyes scanned the individuals in the surgery floor waiting room.

"Yes," replied Cassie, with her hand raised.

"Aah, I just wanted you to know that Mrs. Pearce is now in room 312."

"May we see her?"

"Yes."

"Thank you," said Cassie as she stood up in haste to leave the waiting room, Bob following close behind. Cassie was excited and skeptical, all at the same time, as the pair walked toward the room. *Will she be herself now?*

The door to room 312 was closed part-way, so Cassie peaked around the corner of it to get a glimpse of her mother. She wanted so badly to find her mother smiling at her when she entered the room. But, it wasn't to be so.

Velma was sound asleep. Even though it had been hours since they had given her medication to relax her prior to surgery, she still slept on.

Cassie approached the bed, leaned down and kissed her mother's forehead and whispered, "Mama. It's Cassie. I love you."

To her daughter's great disappointment, Velma did not respond, but continued to sleep. Cassie looked back at her husband, with great distress in her eyes.

"Honey, let's just wait until she wakes up before we make any judgments on her condition," said Bob.

Reluctantly, Cassie agreed. The two pulled chairs up to each side of the bed and just sat there - waiting. Then a gentle knock on the door took their attention to the doorway.

"Pastor Simpson, how are you?"

"I'm just fine, thank you. Stephen called earlier and said that your mother was out of surgery and that everything went well."

"Yes," said Cassie.

Bob got up and offered his chair to the pastor.

"No, thanks. I'm not going to stay long. I just wanted to see if there had been any changes since Stephen's call."

"I'd like to be able to say yes, but she's been asleep since coming out of the recovery area."

"Well, I'm going to scoot on. I have a board meeting this evening and I need to take care of some paperwork before then. I'll be back after the meeting."

"Thank you for coming. I know Mom would be very pleased to see you," said Cassie.

He turned and walked to the door thinking *I can only hope she'll be as anxious to see me as I am to see her. Some people think that because there's snow on the top that there isn't any fire in the hold. They're wrong.* He couldn't help but chuckle at his own thoughts as he walked to the elevator.

The grey-haired, well-dressed gentleman pushed the 'down' button and waited for the elevator. As he stood there, he sighed at the thought of having to write the letter of resignation that he would present to the board that evening. Several draft versions were already on his office computer, but none of them seemed to convey just the right words. *How does one say – 'I quit' – in a nice sorta way?*

A candy-striper holding a box the size of a shoebox walked into Velma's room. "Ma'am, this is the mail for Mrs. Pearce." She set it down on the side table.

Cassie reached over and pulled the box onto her lap. "Bob, this box is full. I mean full to the brim of mail." Cassie began thumbing through the envelopes looking at the return addresses. "Almost all of these are from local people."

"Why don't you open one?"

"I can't. They're addressed to Mama."

"Open just one. Then when the rest of the family gets back, you can decide among yourselves if the rest of the mail should be opened."

"Okay. But just one." She reluctantly took the first one off the pile and opened it. "It says, 'Thinking of You.' Inside, let me see, it says, 'Some things just aren't in our hands, It's tempting to try taking charge and making things right but we know they're best left to God . . . I realize it can be hard, and I hope it helps to know I'm here for you.' It's signed, much love, Carole Blitzer . . . That's so nice. I wonder who she is?"

"It'll be great therapy for your mother to read all of those to her. If she is still not responding after she wakes up, hopefully some word or phrase or even a person's name in one of those cards will trigger something in her mind," prompted Bob.

Cassie was still fingering those envelopes when James and Wanda came into the room.

"Look here, James at all the mail that has come for Mother."

"How nice."

Bob got up from his chair to allow Wanda to sit down. "Where's everyone?"

"We left them at the restaurant. We were finished, so we came on over here to see how Mother is doing," said Wanda.

"She's been asleep this whole time," commented Cassie. "Say, little brother, how's your jaw? I can imagine it's going to be sore for a while. Could you eat anything?"

"Yes, I had some soup." He paused for a moment and then said, "Cassie, the Mexican government is giving us a hard time about letting out information about the Ramirez family."

"Oh."

"I've asked my law partner to keep on it until he breaks through that wall of secrecy there in Mexico City. I'm sure you'll agree, Cassie, that once we find the Ramirez family down there, we can then press them for the money to cover the medical expenses."

"James . . . is that what our mother would want?"

"Cassie, be sensible. Our mother is not able to pursue this legal matter in the state she's in. Someone's gotta do it, and I know you'll agree that I'm the best person to do that with my legal experience and connections."

"James . . . ah . . . the six of us kids are capable of providing Mother with the support and information she needs to take the matter to her own lawyer here in town. Mr. Cranston has been Mama and Daddy's lawyer since I can remember. It's not that we don't believe in your ability to handle such a situation, but I do think we should leave that decision up to her."

"Well, that may be your opinion, but it's not mine. We can't let this get away from us by stalling."

"I'm not stalling, James. I'm just suggesting that we wait until Mother can make her own decisions."

"Well, that may never happen."

"James. Where's your faith?"

"It went by the wayside a long time ago, Sis. I now deal in hard cold facts. Fact one tells me that our mother is still not able to speak for herself. If she continues to be in that state, I will need to go to court to have her judged incompetent to handle her own affairs and then we can get on with the legal matters."

Cassie held back on a reply, afraid of what she might say.

"Fact two, Cassie, is that the kid injured our mother. His mother doesn't have insurance and knows her son is guilty. She'll probably head for the border with him to flee prosecution."

"I'm sorry you feel that way." She looked at her husband, "I think we need to give James and Wanda some time with Mama. Besides that, I could use a cup of coffee." She forced a smile. Two very disheartened people left the room.

Waiting for the elevator, Cassie grabbed Bob's hand, squeezing it hard. Her fingernails dug into the side of his hand until he winced.

"Bob, how can he be so hard and calculating? There's no love there for our mother. He only sees it as another court case whereby he can be the prosecutor who digs up dirt on the accused. And then . . . he made Mother out as incompetent. I'm . . . I'm . . ."

"Hey. Hey. Calm down."

"Whatta ya mean, calm down?"

"Cassie, you're forgetting that God is in control here – not James. If we belittle James for his thinking, we, too, are in error.

"Right now, Cassie, just as you've held onto my hand in desperation, we need to hold to the hand of the One who loves your mother and Who we can trust to bring this to the right conclusion.

"Remember how you felt when our kids were little and one of them would hold tightly to your hand whenever you crossed a busy street?"

She nodded.

"Comforting – huh? Well, I can only imagine that's how God feels when we hold tightly to His hand in the midst of a situation such as this one."

"You're right," she said, as her hand relaxed in his. "I've been acting like a child."

Bob had just leaned over to plant a big kiss on his wife's cheek when the elevator door opened and several people got out. They walked past the couple with a grin on their face in reaction to the loving gesture they had just witnessed. Cassie blushed.

Back in Velma's room, James was seething. "Wanda, I don't understand my family any more. They aren't even considering the exorbitant medical bills that are racking up for Mother. If she needs long-term physical therapy, that will be added expenses. Then there's the possibility that she's never going to be in her right mind – what then?"

"Honey, not so loud."

"What? Am I going to wake up my mother? I thought that would be a good thing."

James continued to rant and rave-on. He walked over to the window and took a deep breath. He saw Cassie and Bob walking toward their car. "Blind. That's what they are – blind."

"James. Come here. Quick."

Continuing to look out the window, he sarcastically asked, "What, Wanda?"

"Honey, your mother is moving and look . . . she opened her eyes."

James whirled around and walked back to Velma's bed. "Well, I'll be! She is awake."

"Well, no one could have slept through your tirade."

"Thanks for the vote of confidence, Wanda."

She paid no attention to what he was saying as she was on her feet and rubbing the back of Velma's hand. "Mother Pearce, it's Wanda."

"I think she heard your voice, James. Why don't you talk to her?"

"Hey, Mother. You've had a good rest." His eyes lit up as he watched his mother turn her head toward him and then she moved her left hand. "Wanda, now you say something. Let's see if she turns toward you."

"Mother, it's Wanda."

"Keep talking," James demanded.

"What'll I say."

"Say anything, even if it's stupid."

"Mother, James and I are here from Portland to see you. You've just had surgery and . . . ."

"Talk louder, Wanda."

"I'm not about to shout."

"Just talk," he said indignantly.

"Cassie and Bob just left to go get some coffee. Are you hungry?" Just then, Velma's head slowly turned in Wanda's direction. "Look. Her head just moved. Now you talk and see if she'll turn back to you."

"Mother, I had surgery here, too. My cheek bone was fractured when the plane I was riding in and . . . look she's turning her head back toward me. Mother, it's James."

"She seems to only be moving her left hand."

"Could be that her right shoulder is hurting from being dislocated, so that keeps her right arm from moving."

"I'm going out to the nurse's station to let them know she's awake."

"Okay, but come right back," he admonished his wife.

Chapter 21

The family members had finished their meals and had left the restaurant, with some to return to the hospital while others had to attend to business elsewhere.

Gordon drove back to work to check on a project that was nearing completion. He would have to sign off on it before it could be shipped off to the customer. So his wife, Trisha rode with Paul and Sandy back to the hospital along with Stephen and Marianne.

As the five walked past the nurse's station, one of the nurses said, "Mr. Pearce, would you mind taking these flowers in to your mother's room?"

There on the counter were three vases of cut flowers and one potted plant. "Hey, I'll need some help with these," quipped Paul.

Walking into Velma's room, the five were a little apprehensive about seeing James again. They were pleasantly surprised to find Velma awake, and that took the edge off the uneasiness they were all feeling. Also, having the flowers in hand made for an opening conversation.

Velma only stared straight ahead as the girls read the cards to her that came with the flowers. Once in a while she made a small movement with her left hand. The scene was hopeful, but also disheartening to the family, but no one expressed it aloud.

James stood up and motioned to Wanda, "We've had our time with Mother, so we're going to go get a cup of coffee now that everyone is back."

At the door, the two encountered Pastor Simpson, who stopped for a moment to greet them as they left. His presence in the room would definitely help to alleviate any lingering uneasiness that the family had been experiencing.

Pastor Simpson looked around the room at all the flowers and said, "My, my, my, it looks like someone has some admirers."

"The flowers from the church are beautiful, Pastor," said Trisha.

"My secretary ordered them. She is good at choosing the right flowers for the right person."

"Pastor, Mother's hand has moved several times. This is such a good sign," said Stephen. "We've all had our turn speaking to her, why don't you come over here and say hello."

The pastor grinned and walked toward the left side of the bed. He laid his hand on top of hers and said, "Hello, Velma. How are you today? So many people from the church have been calling my office to ask how you are doing. You are certainly loved by a lot of people."

Suddenly he gasped as he felt her hand move under his. "Her hand just moved. And look, she's turning her head this way."

With a chuckle, Marianne said, "Pastor, she's heard your voice more in the past several years than any of ours. Three times a week she sits in church listening to your sermons."

"She has also spent a lot of time at the hospital with my wife and me prior to Eva passing away. She has been a good friend to the two of us."

Stephen laid his hand on the pastor's shoulder. "Whenever she speaks of you, it is quite obvious that she thinks quite highly of you."

Pastor Simpson was a little overcome by all that was said and stepped back from the bed. "It appears that she is responding to familiar voices, so let someone else talk with her now."

"Mrs. Ramirez, this is Sgt. Jackson." He was alone in his squad car having just completed duty leading a funeral procession to the cemetery. He had pulled into the parking lot at the police station and decided to give Mrs. Ramirez a call.

"Yes, Sergeant. Hello."

"I was wondering if I could take Tony over to the hospital after I get off work?"

"I don't work today, so I was planning to take him there."

"Oh. Well, since you don't have a car, would it be all right if I picked the two of you up? I'm planning to ask my wife to accompany me there. She knows and works with Mrs. Pearce."

"Well, I guess that would be all right. What time should we be ready?"

"Let's say about four o'clock. I generally get off at 3:30, but sometimes I'm delayed a little."

"That sounds good. We'll be ready. Thank you, sir."

Sgt. Jackson pushed the 'off' button and then speed-dialed his home phone number, hoping his wife would be there. "Hey, sweetheart. How about driving over to see Mrs. Pearce when I get off work? I can pick you up on the way there."

"Yes. I'd like that," she responded.

"Okay. See you around four. How does that sound?"

"Great."

Jack hung up and thought *I hope she doesn't get too angry with me that I'm also picking up the Mrs. Ramirez and Tony. I was afraid if I told her they were going with me that she'd refuse to go. I want her to see that Tony is an okay kid.*

He glanced at the dashboard's digital clock and saw that it was 3:10. *Oops, I gotta get goin'. School lets out in just a couple of minutes.* He started up his police cruiser and began patrolling street-by-street until he reached the Eastside Middle School, his duty route for that afternoon. Students were already climbing aboard a bus or strolling down the street toward home. For some time now, it was noted that police presence at the handful of Middleton schools didn't completely stop gang activity per se, but at least it deterred it at that hour of the day.

As he sat there, his mind wandered for a moment to when he used to pick up his son from school prior to the boy's fatal accident. His thoughts became heavy, but then a voice over the police radio startled him. "Bank robbery in progress at 4th and Pine. Bank employee pushed the silent alarm and then hid in the vault. He says there are two men, both carrying automatic weapons. There are hostages - all lying on the floor."

Sgt. Jackson responded with his badge number and then with the familiar 10-18, which meant he was using lights and siren in responding to the call.

He arrived at the bank and pulled in behind a squad car, one of many on the scene, and got out. He unholstered his duty weapon and made his way to the front line using the parked black-and-whites as cover and concealment.

The first police sergeant on the scene called Jackson and Thomas, on his walkie-talkie to cover the rear exit. Then he called Brady and Farnsworth to cover the east side entrance.

For the next fifteen to twenty minutes, it was a standoff. No movement at all took place. The Chief had now arrived on scene and was given the bank's phone number by Dispatch. He called inside, asking to talk to one of the men. The bank robbers refused to talk with him. He waited a few more minutes and called again. This time his call was answered by an angry voice, "What?"

"If you'll come out with your hands up, no one'll get hurt."

"Oh, sure. I've heard that before. Now, you listen to me, flat-foot. I want a car for safe passage out of here to the airport and I want a plane, gassed up and ready to go when I get there. I'm taking a hostage with me when I leave, to make sure you don't try to stop me. I'll shoot the hostage at the first sign of someone trying to stop us. I don't want to see any snipers on buildings across the street or at the airport either – do ya hear me?"

"You got it."

"Listen, I'm not just talking, I want to see that car here **now** or else I'll start shooting one hostage every fifteen minutes." He turned to look at the bank's clock on the wall, "It's now 4:02. It's your call now, copper."

He hung up before the Chief could respond. If the Chief had an opportunity, he would have used some type of persuasive dialogue in hopes of trying to defuse the situation. Instead, he looked at his watch and saw that twenty minutes had elapsed since arriving on the scene. Now there were only fifteen minutes before the robbers would begin carrying out their threat. He turned and asked one of his men, "Is the negotiator here, yet?"

"Carlton just pulled in, Chief."

The Chief had been with the Middleton Police Department since he was a young man, becoming the chief three years ago. He had handled bank robberies before, but was never as good a hostage negotiator as the man they had hired. "The guy's a wonder," he often said after an incident whereby the negotiator had to intervene. "Sure glad he's on our team."

"Carlton, glad to see you, man," said the Chief, as he glanced at his watch. "4:05, that means we have only twelve more minutes before his threat is carried out."

"Whatta we got in there?"

"Well, there's an bank employee hid out inside the vault and he's described the two suspects as one white male in his twenties and one black male in his forties. They both are wearing blue jeans, dark blue or black sweatshirts with hoods and dirty white tennis shoes.

"The white male has a dragon tattoo on the back of his right hand. The younger of the two seems to be in charge and he's pretty hot-tempered. They've got automatic rifles and have all the hostages on the floor. I tried reaching him twice and the second time he said he would kill one hostage every fifteen minutes until we first get him a vehicle to drive to the airport and secondly a plane gassed and ready for take-off. He plans to take a hostage with him for security. I guess that's about all I can tell you."

"Okay. Thanks, Chief," said Carlton, as he checked his watch.

Carlton's primary objective now is to prolong the situation. He was well trained and knew that the longer a hostage situation lasts, the more likely that it will end peacefully. With the given timeline of fifteen minutes now down to eight, he must use stall tactics to push back the deadline proclaimed by the criminals.

His second objective is to foster a relationship between the bank robber and the hostages. He must convince the hostage-taker to allow medical treatment or the release of sick or injured hostages. Those hostages could provide invaluable information as to the locations and habits of the captors.

If no one is released, then he would need to negotiate the delivery of medicine, food and water. The food would be delivered to the bank in bulk packages and have to be prepared – thus allowing more time to pass.

Carlton knew from the Chief's phone call to the captors that they were angry. So now his job was to stall and also make a counter-offer with the hostage taker. He checked his digital watch and was then ready to begin negotiating. "Captain, what's the phone number in there?"

Chapter 22

At the Ramirez apartment at a couple of minutes to four, both Tony and Consuela were ready to leave for the hospital.

"Tony, it's almost four. Keep an eye out the window for Sgt. Jackson's vehicle."

"Okay."

While he did that, she went to the kitchen to put some plastic wrap around the stem of some chrysanthemums that she purchased from the corner mom-and-pop grocery store. She had placed them in water until they were ready to leave. Now, after wrapping up the flowers, she took a long deep sniff of their fragrance and walked to the sofa where she had placed her purse and keys.

"He's late, Mama."

"Be patient, son. He may have had a last minute phone call at the station."

"Do you think Mrs. Pearce will like the flowers?"

"Tony, most women love flowers, no matter what kind they are. There's just something about a woman receiving flowers that brings such pleasure to her. Remember that, son, when you get married someday."

Tony laughed. "Mama, I don't even have a girlfriend."

"Just you wait, son." She checked her watch and Sgt. Jackson was now ten minutes late. She sat down on the sofa to wait.

≈

Meanwhile, at the Jackson household, Connie was getting ready to go to the hospital, anticipating the opportunity to see her friend, Velma. She pulled on her panty-hose, slipped her size six feet into her shoes and then checked herself in the full-length mirror that hung from the bedroom door. *I hope she's better today* she thought as she whirled around to see the back of her outfit. *We need Velma back at work. She seems to be the one person who can bring comfort to those kids. I've learned a lot from her, but I still have a long ways to go before I'll ever be an exceptional advocate like she is.* She checked her watch. *I'd better be standing on the front porch when he drives up. I know how punctual he likes everything and everyone to be.*

At 4:30 when Jack had not shown up, she fished around in her purse to find her cell phone to call the police station. If Jack was late, he probably had something come up at the last minute. *No sense standing out here if he's not able to get off work right now.*

The desk sergeant answered the phone and informed Connie that Jack was on a call and she probably wouldn't be able to contact him on his cell phone. She started to ask questions, but knew that he probably wouldn't divulge any information about what kind of call her husband was responding to. She turned and went back into the house. *Responding to a call - that could mean a domestic dispute, a traffic accident or something even worse. Hmm, I wonder what it is?*

Earlier in their marriage, she would become frantic wondering if he could get hurt or even worse – get killed -

while answering a call. But, she had learned over the years not to second-guess where her husband could be and just know that he was a good cop who knew what he was doing.

Connie went back into the house, kicked off her high heels, grabbed a bottle of water from the refrigerator and then sat down in her recliner to watch the last few minutes of her favorite talk show.

Back at the Ramirez apartment, Consuela said to Tony, "I guess Sgt. Jackson's not coming. He seems like such a nice man, so he'll probably let us know later why he couldn't come by for us."

"I suppose." The disappointment showed on his face.

She was almost relieved that they weren't going to the hospital. Facing Mrs. Pearce's family would probably have meant that she would have to listen to accusations about her son and she would, of course, need to defend him.

She got up and walked to the kitchen to put the flowers back into a vase of water and began to prepare an early dinner. With Tony so upset over the past few days she had earlier baked him a chocolate cake - his favorite.

At five o'clock at the Jackson home, Connie switched channels to watch the early news broadcast. The first thing that came on was the large print words: NEWS BULLETIN. So much ugliness was going on in the world today that she thought that could mean another war had broken out in some country in the Middle East. But, the news anchor said, "A hostage situation has taken place at the First National Bank of Middleton. Two armed men entered the bank around three fifteen this afternoon and are holding a dozen individuals hostage. Police have surrounded the bank and we believe a hostage negotiator is on the scene in hopes of convincing the bank robbers not to carry out their threat to kill a hostage every fifteen minutes."

Connie was spellbound as she watched and listened to the details of the robbery. *That's why he's late. He participated years ago in the standoff of a bank robbery here in Middleton, so he knows what he's doing. I can only believe those bank robbers will give themselves up.*

Just then her phone rang. "Hello."

"Connie. This is Sandra. Do you have the news on?"

"Yes, Sandra. Our husbands are probably there on the scene."

"Yes, but what if those robbers come out shooting. One of our husbands might get killed."

"Oh, come on, Sandra. You know better than that. You've been a policeman's wife for how many years now?"

"Ah . . . nine."

"Your husband and mine are well trained. The best thing you can do is turn off the TV and go start his dinner. Fix him something special – something he really likes."

"Suppose you're right."

"Sandra, you know they probably have a hostage-negotiator on the scene, who will do his best to defuse the situation. Now, what is Terry's favorite meal?"

"Hungarian goulash."

"How do you make it?" Connie knew how to make the dish, but hoped that changing the subject from the bank situation to food would help calm Sandra down.

The two gals talked for a few more minutes and then hung up to go fix dinner.

As Connie stood at the kitchen counter she thought about the conversation with Sandra, *wow, the same tactics that the hostage-negotiator uses, is almost the same as what the CASA/GAL program teaches us to use when it's necessary. I guess I am learning. Surprise! Surprise!*

She smiled as she walked to the refrigerator to look and find what she might fix for dinner. She had not planned anything, hoping that they would stop and get something to eat on their way home from the hospital. Her mind was somewhere else as she stood there gazing intently into the refrigerator; her eyes not really fixed on anything in particular. Suddenly, a chill went through her from the cold of the refrigerator and she shivered. *Oh, let me see what we've got here.*

As Connie went about fixing dinner, she thought about her friend, Velma, and what it was that made her so special. *She has such a knack for loving people. I guess it isn't a knack but really a gift that I guess God has given her. She speaks of God with great reverence and I believe she has such closeness to Him that it shows in her everyday life. I don't think I've ever been around someone like her.*

She doesn't belittle people, even the grotesque people who we deal with that harm little kids. She even told me once that she takes time to pray for the riffraff that we have to associate ourselves with. Well, she didn't use that term, but that kind of lowlife shouldn't be given the time of day. How does she do it is beyond my comprehension.

Deep in thought, she jumped when the phone rang. "Hello."

"Connie, I'm sorry that I couldn't get there to pick you up. We're . . . ah . . ."

Connie interrupted him. "I know. I saw it on TV. Are you all right?"

"Sure. I can't talk but a moment, but I wanted to let you know that I may be here for a while. The negotiator has done a terrific job so far in giving us more time to work out this situation. The bank robber has gone far past the time limit in his demand for safe passage out of the bank."

"Good. Sandra called. She's so worried about Terry."

"He's okay. We're just standing our ground here, keeping our presence visual to those guys inside the bank. So far, so good. The negotiator has been able to stall for time and no one has been killed.

"Give Sandra a call. Tell her not to worry."

"I will. Take care of yourself."

"You can bet on that. I love you, Connie."

"I love you, too, Jack. I'll see you in a little while."

Chapter 23

In the corner of the lobby of the bank, huddled together, was a husband and wife possibly in their late seventies or early eighties. The older hostage-taker stood near them and could hear them praying. A twinge of guilt ran through him, remembering how his grandmother had prayed with him as a child when he retired for the night. *Those people must be Christians* he surmised.

His dad had left his mother when he was three years old and then one day she walked out too, never to return. He and his baby sister were left there alone until someone noticed a child crying and called the police. The young boy was able to tell the police his grandmother's name, and she came to pick up the two children at the police station. They would live with her for the next ten years. She died and then the two were sent to separate foster homes. All those memories came pouring back into the warped mind of the bank robber.

His grandmother was the only person on earth who showed him love. *She would bundle up Sis, still a tiny thing, and we would walk the ten blocks to the little church service that was held inside an old used-car salesroom.* As he now stood in front of that elderly couple, he recalled the songs they sang and the smiles on all the faces.

Then he felt the end of the barrel of his partner's gun in his ribs. "Hey, pay attention to what you're doin'. You look like you're day-dreamin'. That's one way of getting into trouble." He turned and walked away.

"Sorry." The older began to walk around the room, and as he did he looked down into the distraught faces of the people lying or sitting on the floor. He came to a pregnant lady who was rubbing her large belly. Once again his mind momentarily went back to when his mother was pregnant with his sister. She would have him put his little hand on her stomach to feel the baby kicking. He recalled that each time he felt that movement he would giggle.

He turned and quickly walked away. *Those other robberies we pulled didn't involve older people and pregnant women. This has gone too far.*

The younger thief, his finger still on the trigger of his gun, stood ready to shoot at a moment's notice. From time to time, he would turn to look out the huge front window at the crowd that had gathered out there. Television cameras were set up and a woman stood holding her child tightly against her body. An ambulance was ready in case of a medical emergency. And then there were the cops – *yup, there's still cops galore out there.* The bank phone rang and it startled him. He looked up at the large clock on the wall and then said, "I knew they would call. This time they'd better be telling me the car is ready."

"Is the car here?" he demanded, his first words after picking up the phone.

"It's here," said the negotiator. "But . . . um . . . we're sending police cars out to every intersection on the way to the airport to stop traffic. You'll have a clear shot to the airport when that's all done. Give me another ten minutes or so to get them in place."

"You'd better not be stalling me. I've already picked out the first person to get a bullet between the eyes. She's a pretty young thing." As he spoke, he turned to point his gun in her direction. "She's pregnant! Yes, pregnant. I'll call you back in ten minutes." He hung up the phone and whirled around to face the panicked hostages who had overheard his conversation.

The young pregnant woman had both of her hands covering her mouth to keep from screaming. Tears gushed from her eyes.

The older hostage-taker gasped in disbelief that this so-called 'pal of his' could do something that despicable. He looked over at the older couple who had been praying. They sat with arms around each other in a state of shock. *I can't let him do this. I've got to stop him.*

The older couple had begun to pray - out loud. The younger thief looked around the room at everyone who now had bowed their heads in prayer. "What's going on here? You think that I'll be nice guy if you pray. Well, you've got another thing coming." He pointed his gun in the direction of the elderly lady and said to her husband, "Mister, if you don't stop your praying, I'm going to show you that your God isn't in control here. I am. Do you hear me? I am!" He waved his gun in her face. "She'll be a dead lady before you know it."

The older perpetrator's heart was pounding now as he made his way ever so slowly around the perimeter of the room to come up behind his younger partner, trying not to be conspicuous.

The younger one moved from person to person, pointing his gun at them. Then he leaned over to shove his gun in the face of a young well-dressed man in a business suit sitting on the floor. Before he could say a word, the black man raised the butt of his gun up high and brought it quickly down on the back of his partner's head. The young one fell to the floor and the older of the two, still holding his gun, reached down on the floor and grabbed up the automatic rifle that had fallen out of his partner's hand.

Everyone sat frozen, believing they now faced a man with a gun in each hand.

To their astonishment, he quickly turned to a couple of the men and said, "Find something and tie him up. I'm going to the front door to surrender." He handed the two guns to another man and said, "Here you take these. I won't need 'em where I'm going. I'd rather go to prison for armed robbery than for murder." He slowly walked to the front door; all the while the hostages sat in shock for what had just transpired.

"Hold your fire. I'm coming out," he shouted, as he opened the door. "I'm unarmed.

The Chief and negotiator looked at one another in amazement. Then the Chief yelled out, "Come away from the door. Turn around and back up. Where's your pal?"

"He's tied up."

"Tied up?"

"Yes. I asked two of the men to tie him up. He can't hurt anyone anymore," he yelled, as he slowly walked backwards.

"Now, get down on your knees with your hands over your head," shouted the Chief.

The man obeyed. Two policemen ran forward; one cuffed him while the other one patted him down to check for weapons.

Hostages ran from the building. Some to waiting loved ones, others to get as far away from the building as they could get.

The police entered the building and found the young hostage-taker tied up and sitting in the middle of the lobby floor.

"Here's the guns," said one of the male hostages. "I can't believe it's over. This guy's partner is the hero. He brought the younger guy down."

"Stick around for a few minutes, if you will. We'll need your statement on those facts."

"Sure. Be glad to."

The young would-be robber was escorted out the door by two policemen. The crowd shouted and jeered as he was placed in a squad car.

With his hand stuck out to shake hands with Carlton, the Chief said, "You did it again, Carlton. Thanks, my friend. I know those hostages are grateful for what you've done here today."

"Hey Chief, it's my job. I can't say that I'm not proud of the work that's been done here, but it was really teamwork between all of us and all of them in there."

"Let's go home," said the Chief. "Oh no, here come the TV reporters. That means I need to put on my fake smile and answer their countless questions."

"Smile," yelled one of his own men, "You may be on Candid Camera."

He grinned, and said, "Aah, go home."

The yellow crime-scene tape had now cordoned off the front of the bank, and no one was allowed inside, only the police. Police detectives were inside questioning some of the hostages' and their other co-workers were outside taking down hostage statements.

The young pregnant woman, who was discovered to be one of the bank tellers, was placed in an ambulance and taken to the hospital for observation.

The older couple, who had been praying, was greeted by a younger couple, probably family members. They were hugged and held tight, longer than was usual.

The television reporters finished their interviews with the police chief, bank president, bank employees and several witnesses. They were now packing up the cameras to head back to the studio.

Before leaving the parking lot, Sgt. Jackson called Mrs. Ramirez to apologize for not meeting his appointment with her. He only said that he had to handle a situation downtown that took longer than he had anticipated. He said that he'd call the next day to make arrangements to take Tony to the hospital.

By six o'clock the parking lot was empty - a far cry from the scene earlier.

Chapter 24

Visiting hours were over at the hospital and the Pearce family had said their goodbyes to their mother and went home. Cassie and Bob, Paul and Sandy were all staying out at Velma's home. Those spare bedrooms were now getting some good use.

For Cassie, she loved her old bedroom where Velma had placed her daughter's favorite Raggedy Ann and Cabbage Patch dolls on a high shelf. Whenever Cassie occupied that room she would lie there in bed and smile lovingly at her old friends as she recalled those younger days of her life.

James and Wanda would stay one more night at the motel and then, after a doctor's appointment the next morning, they would drive back to Portland in the rental car. Wanda had an open-ended airline ticket, but they had decided not use it until they returned later in the month for another doctor's appointment.

The night before at the motel, James said to Wanda, "Can't wait to get back to the office and sink my teeth into this travesty that my family is allowing to happen to Mother. They're all so blinded to what Mother really needs. I'll show them."

Stephen had decided to go to work that morning, planning to visit his mother on his lunch hour and again after work. In a few weeks, it would be final exam time for his students and he wanted to be in the classroom to begin prepping them for it. He knew that his wife, Marianne, and other family members would be there at the hospital to continue a running dialogue with his mother.

Gordon, too, had decided to go to work that morning, promising his siblings to visit their mom as soon as he got off work.

That morning found Pastor Simpson standing alone beside Velma's bed soon after her breakfast time. She was awake and only turned her head in his direction after talking to her at some length.

"Velma, I told the board last night that I am retiring. Can you believe that, Velma? I'm actually gonna retire? They were all very nice about it, with Sam Goldsmith trying to convince me to wait a while. But, I told them that I had already turned in my resignation to the district office and they had accepted it. I can't imagine what I'm going to do with my time. Sure hope you're going to be up and around soon, as I'll need a friend to walk the beach with me."

Velma moved her hand, which caught the attention of her pastor. He stopped talking, but then decided that he should keep rattling on to see if his voice was actually making a difference.

He stared down at her as he continued a barrage of words that he wasn't paying attention to what he was saying. They were only words. When she blinked her eyes he talked even more.

He'd been there in her room for over a half-hour and decided it was time to get back to the church office. As he was leaving, Sonja came down the hallway toward Velma's room. He greeted her with a hug and then told her he needed to get back to the office.

Sonja had called her cousin that morning before leaving for the hospital. She wanted her aunt, Velma's sister in San Antonio, to speak by phone to Velma and asked her cousin to arrange to have her mother at home when the call was placed.

She had awakened during the night and that idea was so strong on her mind. She was willing to try anything that would trigger her mother's mind, and hopefully she would recognize her own sister's voice.

"Hi Mama. It's Sonja. Did you have a good night's sleep? You look rested.

"Mama, I'm going to get your sister on the phone. Okay?" She scrolled down on her cell phone and pressed her aunt's name. "Ah, cell phones. What would we do without them?

"Good morning. This is Sonja. Is your mama there? . . . Okay . . . Great!" She placed her cell phone against Velma's ear and waited. She saw no reaction, but continued to be patient. Her earlier phone call to her cousin explained that her aunt needed to keep talking even if Velma did not respond. It was her voice that was important in trying to get Velma's attention.

"Who is that, Mama?"

Sonja noticed that her mother's eyes were moving back and forth. Something she had not been doing over the past two days.

Sonja took the phone away from her mother's ear just for a moment to say, "Auntie, please keep talking. Her eyes moved. I think she recognizes your voice." Sonja again placed the phone next to her mother's ear.

Sonja's mouth dropped open when she saw her mother's mouth open and move as though she was saying something. She put her ear down next to her mother's mouth to try and make out if she was actually talking or just mumbling.

"Maaaary . . . Maaaary," she said, barely above a whisper and hardly moving her lips.

"Yes, Mama. It's your sister Mary on the phone."

"Maaaary . . . Maaaary."

Sonja put the phone up to her own ear and said, "Aunt Mary she's calling your name. Did you hear her? Please keep talking to her."

"Maaaary." Her eyes began to roll from side to side, and she lifted her left hand in the direction of the phone that was against her ear and then brought it back down.

"Maaaary."

"Yes, Mother. It's Mary. Is she talking to you?"

This time, when her hand went up to her ear she moved her fingers to feel the instrument.

Sonja cried, "Thank you, Lord." She was so astounded and could hardly believe what was happening right before her eyes. She wanted to run and shout to everyone to come and see for themselves.

Knowing how difficult it must be for her aging aunt to talk to her incapacitated sister for very long, Sonja decided to end the call. "Aunt Mary, it's wonderful. She heard your voice, dear, and recognized that it was you. That's the first sign of any kind of response since her accident. Thank you for talking to her. Sure . . . I'll keep you informed on how she's doing. I love you. . . . Bye."

Sonja sat down in the chair beside her mother's bed, still exhilarated by this stunning progress. She scrolled down to Marianne's name on her cell phone, pressed it and it rang and rang. "Oh no, she's not home." She hung on for a few more rings and then, "Marianne. I almost hung up. I thought you weren't home. You won't believe what just happened. I called Aunt Mary and had her talk to Mama. After a few minutes Mama said, 'Maaary' real slow and barely moved her lips. She repeated the name over and over. Marianne, I believe this is the first sign that Mother's mind is recovering.

"Yes, Marianne, thank God. He heard us, didn't He? I'm just sorry that everyone couldn't be here to experience this new development with me.

"I need to call Cassie over at Mama's house and she can share the news with Paul and Sandy. Then I'll let Trisha know about it so that she can share it with Gordon. Forgive me for talking so fast. I can't remember when I've been this excited. I'll talk to you later. Bye."

Sonja's calls to Cassie and Trisha were just as exuberant and animated, with her hands waving in the air as she talked.

A nurse entered the room to take Velma's vital signs and saw the change in her patient immediately. She smiled at Sonja and said, "Her doctor will be thrilled."

The next call was to James and Wanda. She had prayed on her way to the hospital that the Lord would help keep her calm when she talked with or was around her younger brother. If she had her own way, she would give him a piece of her mind, but this wasn't the time for that.

She called, but it just rang. No answer. When the voicemail kicked in she said, "Good news, little brother. Mother talked with her sister this morning." She left it at that, determining to share the whole story with him when he either called back or came to the hospital.

Sonja sat quietly by as a nurse gave her mother a bath. She wanted to see if Velma would respond in any way with the nurse. A one-way conversation by the nurse with Velma took place all during her bath. Sonja witnessed that Velma's eyes, still a bit glassy, would follow the nurse whenever she moved from one side of the bed to the other. She also spotted a slight wiggling of her mother's fingers on her left hand while her arm was being cleansed.

Soon after Velma's bath was completed, her eyelids became heavy and she was soon asleep. Sonja gasped at first, but then realized she was just sleeping.

James and Wanda walked into the room. "Got your message, Sonja. So tell me about the call to Aunt Mary."

"Sure, little brother."

"Will you stop calling me that. We're adults now, let's talk like adults."

Sonja wanted to fire back, but restrained herself from saying anything negative. She had determined that the positive progress of her mother was to be the focus of the conversation.

"I called Aunt Mary this morning to have her talk with Mama. At first, Mama showed no movement in her eyes or her body. Then her lips slightly moved and I put my head down near her mouth to listen. She was saying, 'Maaaary'

– ever so slowly. She kept repeating it over and over again as her eyes moved back and forth. I wanted to jump for joy."

"Well, she doesn't look very lively at this moment."

"She just fell asleep a few minutes ago. I know you'll be as excited as I am when she wakes up. Say, what was the result of your doctor's appointment?"

"He said everything looks fine. I need to come back and see him in a month. After that, should I have any problems, I'll seek the advice of my own doctor in Portland."

"Looks like you're able to move your jaw more." Sonja turned toward Wanda and smiled. "That's good news. It appears that this is going to be a good day for the Pearce family."

"Sonja, we aren't going to hang around. We just came to see Mother one more time before we head back to Portland. I have an upcoming case that needs my attention."

"Oh. Are you sure you don't want to wait and talk to Mama?"

"I'll call her tonight."

"Okay," said Sonja, saddened at his complacent attitude.

James gave Sonja a quick hug and a peck on the cheek, saying, "See ya soon."

Wanda also gave her a hug and the two left the room without saying a goodbye to Velma.

Tears formed in Sonja's eyes, so bewildered at the smug attitude of her brother. She heaved a big sigh and then sat down in the chair beside her mother's bed. "Mama, what has to happen to bring James back to his senses? I guess only God has the answer to that question. I know you've prayed for him for years and so has the rest of our family. So, even though it looks like there's no hope for James, there really is!"

Velma slept on.

After Tony left for school, Consuela poured herself another cup of coffee and sat down on the sofa to watch the morning news on the local talk show program. She was taken aback by the photos showing the bank robbery from the night before. There was Sgt. Jackson with his weapon drawn. Further photos showed him again when one of the bank robbers came out the front door to give himself up.

"So that's what he was doin' yesterday. Hmm. I guess I shouldn't be so skeptical about his relationship with Tony. Instead, I should be pleased that such a man like him would take an interest in my son. Tony could use some male influence. All that he's really aware of in life is from my female perspective. That sure won't help him when he graduates and goes out into society."

Salt in an Unsavory World

Chapter 25

It was now Friday and day five since Velma's accident and some of the out-of-town family members had to decide whether they should stay or go home. For the most part, Paul and Sandy, along with Cassie and Bob, agreed that their mother was beginning to make progress and they talked of leaving that afternoon. They had been absent from their respective jobs since Monday.

James and Wanda had already left on Thursday in the rental car, requesting that they be kept apprised of Velma's condition.

Pastor Simpson was in his office early that morning. A two-day revival meeting at his church was planned for Saturday evening and Sunday morning and evening. A guest speaker was invited to bring the three different messages, but Peter Simpson also felt the need to share something with the parishioners about Velma's accident and recovery.

He knew that he would have to put down on paper what he would say as his emotions regarding Velma were now on his sleeve. Worst come to worst, he could read what needed to be said. He sat down at his computer. But before he typed the first word, he bowed his head over the keyboard and prayed. *Lord, I sense in my spirit that You would have me speak to the congregation to encourage them to believe that You will touch the life of Velma Pearce. I feel that there is fear among my congregation and*

I need to quell those negative thoughts. I can only do this with the help of Your Holy Spirit. Thank you, Lord. Amen.

He felt a peace in his spirit and began to type as the words came to him:

>Velma Pearce lies in the Middleton General Hospital after an accident that she didn't see coming. We, as Christians, sometimes believe that faith will help us escape difficulties in life because we are the Children of God and that His angels will follow us all the time protecting us from *all* harm. Not always so!
>
>Everyone, not just Christians, was given a measure of faith when they were born. That type of faith is produced when we sit down in a chair and hope that it holds us up. We fly in a plane in the hands of a pilot believing he will get us safely to our destination.
>
>But, in reality, the spiritual kind of faith is only received at the time someone accepts Christ as Savior. Faith is the endurance to wait and see through either the good or the difficult circumstances, to their conclusion. We may never see the actual workings of God in all cases, but we must hold on until God has completed and brought His will into fruition.
>
>Noah took one-hundred-twenty years to build an ark to God's specifications and instructions. He was mocked and ridiculed the entire time he was constructing what some might have called a monstrosity and going - nowhere. But, Noah had

faith to believe in what God had told him and that it *would* come to pass in God's timing.

Velma Pearce has selflessly served the Lord for many years. In the past decade, or so, she has spent her time working here at our church at whatever she was asked to do. She's been there when food was needed for the family of a deceased member of our congregation. She sewed costumes for the Christmas pageant. And she has also given tirelessly to her work as an advocate for children in our community who are victims of abuse or neglect.

Velma Pearce does not look at the harsh reality of a wayward child as hopeless. No, indeed not. That child may have had a run-in with the police after stealing food for his family because his insensitive, drug-addicted parents did not provide for him. Velma never looks at the circumstances, but looks to God, asking 'Lord, what would You have me to do to help this child to become a productive, moral and decent human-being?'

You are well aware of the good she does in our local community. Velma Pearce can be called *salt in an* . . .

He stopped typing. *I can't say that. They'll think I'm playing favorites.* He pressed the backspace key to erase that sentence. Then he began again.

But, Velma Pearce is only one among many of you in our church who can be called *salt in an unsavory world,* today. This type of person makes a big difference in the lives of many.

He again stopped typing, as tears had formed and he couldn't see the screen. He reached in his pocket for his handkerchief, lifted up his eye glasses and dried his eyes. He inhaled and let it out slowly, and then continued to type.

I've been asked by some of you, 'Why is it that Velma has worked so tirelessly to help young children, but then God allowed a young child to cause the accident that put her in the hospital?'

I can't answer that question. I only know that God teaches us in His Word to look not at the circumstances, but to look to Him.

You are familiar with the story in the thirteenth chapter of the Book of Numbers where God commanded Moses to send twelve of his men to spy on and explore the land of Canaan. God had promised that land to the Israelites.

Ten of those spies returned with a report that the situation was too insurmountable for the Israelites to tackle. In other words, their eyes were on the circumstances that they witnessed. On the other hand, Joshua and Caleb spoke encouragingly. They admitted the stature and strength of the people were seemingly overwhelming, but they were far from despairing. Their response was one of faith, even though the situation seemed too great for them to maneuver without the Hand of God. They would need to call on Him for help.

Now is the time for you and me to take that same stand in waiting for God to move in our beloved sister's life. If it's God's timing for Velma Pearce to go home to be with Him, then so be it, and we'll praise Him for it. But, in the meantime we must believe with her family that God is a life-giver and in His sovereignty he can touch her body and make it whole.

Instead of asking why, why, why, we should be asking that our faith be increased to believe for Velma's healing.

Peter Simpson sat back in his chair, his head bowed. Then he took off his glasses, leaned his elbows on his desk and buried his face into his hands. He seemed to be drained of all emotion at that moment.

He did sense, though, that what he'd just said on the screen of his computer *was* from his heart and also from the heart of God. He sat up straight, took hold of the mouse, pointed the cursor to the 'print' icon and then hit 'enter'.

He picked up the sheets of paper as the printer spewed them out and placed them in the top drawer of his desk for safekeeping until the next day.

Unknowingly to Pastor Simpson, his secretary was standing in the open doorway as he spoke aloud, "Brother Calloway, before you bring your message, I need to speak to my congregation."

"Who are you talking to?" She had noticed that no one else was in the room

"Oh, I'm talkin' to myself – again. You know how us ol' codgers are, we don't have to have someone to speak to

- we just go right on jawing. If you must know, Mrs. French, I plan to speak to the congregation tomorrow evening before Brother Calloway begins his message."

"How formal we are today, calling me Mrs. French. What is so important that it can't wait until after the revival services?"

"It's about Velma Pearce."

"Oh."

"I feel that it's important that all of our people believe for her healing. What I sense that God wants me to do is to put down the spirit of fear that has stymied the faith of our parishioners. Some have a difficult time believing for an older person to be healed. 'Why doesn't God just take them Home?' some will ask.

"Okay. I understand. It's a good idea."

"Why, thank you, Sarah, for that accolade." He smiled and she returned his smile.

Sarah French, in her mid-sixties, had been his secretary for twelve years and her husband was the maintenance man. Pastor Simpson relied heavily on them both and considered them to be his friends. They understood and respected each other.

Both out-of-town couples decided that they should start for home and leave their mother completely in the hands of God. It wasn't an easy decision for either Cassie or Paul, but one that they felt at peace about.

Velma was responding on this day just as she had been the day before. Her eyes moved about, especially when someone spoke to her. Her left hand moved around, as she seemed to be feeling of different items; the blanket, the pillow, and she even tugged at the top of her hospital gown.

Cassie called Pastor Simpson to say they were leaving for Seattle and Paul to Walla Walla. "Pastor, Bob and I would have loved to be in the revival services this weekend with you, but we really need to get back to Seattle."

"I understand, child. I'm pleased that you called because I want you to know that I am retiring from the pastorate at the end of the month. I will be telling my congregation that news on Sunday morning.

"I will have plenty of time on my hands and would be more than happy to attend to your mother during the day whenever she goes home. She was there for me when I needed someone to help care for my wife before we called in hospice.

"Cassie, may I share with you something else that is very personal?"

"Of course."

"Cassie, this may sound a little strange and I hope not too ridiculous coming from an old man."

"Pastor, I've known you since I was a teenager and so appreciate you in your capacity not only as a preacher, but also as a family friend. Whatever it is that you tell me, I will guard it with all diligence."

"Cassie, I . . . ah . . . I have feelings for your mother more than just as her pastor. I recognized that development the first day she was in the hospital, as I looked down into her face. My heart was broken that this woman I really cared for might not live long enough for me to tell her so. I hope I haven't been too presumptuous in sharing my feelings for her with you."

"Oh, Pastor Simpson, I couldn't be more pleased to know that I can return to Seattle and leave my mother here in the hands of a trusting family friend. You have my blessings."

"Thank you, my dear. Your opinion is very important to me. I hope I'm not being too overconfident to believe your mother would consider me as a beau."

"Oh, Pastor. My mother has always held you in high regard. I'm pretty sure she will be honored to have you be a part of her life."

"Thank you, Cassie. You are very reassuring. I sometimes feel like I'm a young teenager falling for his first girlfriend."

Cassie laughed. "Oh, that's wonderful."

"Cassie, I would be pleased if you would inform your brothers and sister of my disclosure and share with them that I will be more than happy to assist the family in caring for your mother when she is released from the hospital. I would consider that as a big favor to me."

"You can be sure that our family will feel as I do about the situation. Pastor Simpson, God bless you as you retire and may the Lord continue to guide you in whatever He shows you to do with your life. Much love from both Bob and me."

"Thank you, Cassie. I love you, too."

Peter Simpson sighed as he sat back in his chair. It was such a relief to be able to tell the Pearce family about his feelings for their mother.

———

Chapter 26

A knock came at Consuela Ramirez's apartment door. "Who could that be this early in the morning?" She looked through the peephole, but did not recognize the man who stood on the porch.

She left the security door-chain attached and opened the door a crack. "May I help you?"

"I'm from the Middleton Daily News and I wondered if I might speak to you for just a moment?"

"About what?"

"I was at the scene of the accident where your son hit Mrs. Pearce and I just wanted to get your side of the story."

"No, I'd rather not talk about it."

"I'll just take a couple of minutes of your time. I just want to verify the details that I've already gathered. Your help in that matter would be very important to this case."

Reluctantly, Consuela unchained the door and opened it. She did not let him come in, but she went out on the small porch landing and closed the door behind her. It was cold, so she pulled her sweater tightly around her while she proceeded to talk with the man.

"How did you find my home?" she asked.

"Um, as I said before I was there at the scene of the accident. I overheard your son telling the policeman his name and address. My purpose in coming here today is to make sure that your son's side of the story gets told."

"I see. And what may I ask will you do with that?"

"I plan to have it printed in our evening paper."

"My son is a good boy. He would never hurt anyone. He said that when he rode past the lady, she stepped out a little and his handlebar caught her arm. It wasn't his fault."

"If they find him guilty, you do realize you'll be responsible for the lady's medical bills."

Consuela's hand went to her mouth. "Oh, no. That can't be."

"Yes, it can. Her insurance company will contact your insurance company for all her medical expenses."

"I don't have any insurance."

"Wow, lady. Sounds like you're in deep trouble."

"I can't talk anymore. Please leave!" she said and went inside. She slammed the door behind her and laid her back against the door in utter dismay of what she had just heard.

Sure enough the young man's article was front page news that evening. If the citizens of Middleton thought that Velma Pearce's accident was headline news earlier in the week, this article brought even more attention to her state of affairs.

A young housewife fixing the evening meal sat down for a moment to scan the front page of the newspaper that she had just retrieved from the front porch. She couldn't help but notice the large print headline which read: **Child Advocate in Dire Straits**. She scanned the article and then put the paper down, aghast at what she'd read.

"I can't believe this is happening to Mrs. Pearce. Why?"

Tonja happened to be one of the first children who Velma had befriended as an advocate for the court. Without her help, the young girl at that time would still be living in a home with her sex-offender father, who was unknown to the police at that time. Her mother had disappeared into thin air, leaving the child to fend for herself. School officials stepped in when Tonja did not attend school for over a week. With some help from Child Welfare, Tonja was taken from her home and placed in foster care.

Velma met Tonja a week later and the two bonded immediately. The young girl was never fortunate enough to have a grandmother, at least that she knew of. With the caring attitude that her advocate showed, she immediately took to the older woman.

Tonja lived with foster parents until she completed high school and went on to the University of Washington in Seattle to pursue a degree in journalism. Now, she was a wife and mother of an infant child. When the baby was born, Velma was one of the first visitors at the hospital to see the infant.

Tonja now sat on her sofa, the newspaper crumpled beside her and a jumble of thoughts running through her mind. But mainly she knew she must become an advocate for her special friend, Velma Pearce.

She smelled something burning on the stove and ran to the kitchen to retrieve a pot of potatoes that had cooked dry and was now burnt. "Oh, well. I'll fix rice instead."

It was difficult to keep her mind on preparing the rest of the meal and even through dinner her husband noticed how preoccupied she seemed to be. "Hon, what's the matter? You seem so distant."

Tonja shared her news about Velma Pearce with her husband.

His comment was, "Sweetie, there's nothing you can do about it. Just stay out of other people's business."

"That's all and good for you to say. Mrs. Pearce was the one who was there for me when I was a frightened child sent to live with strangers. Yes, they did turn out to be wonderful foster parents to me, but in all actuality, it was Mrs. Pearce who took the time to make sure I didn't have to go back and live with my father."

"Well, heed my words. Stay out of it," he said slowly and deliberately.

Tonja moved her food around her plate with her fork, hearing what he was saying, but knowing full well that she could not let this matter go by the wayside.

The next morning after Tonja's husband had left for work, the baby fed, bed made and dishes washed, she sat down at her computer. She first typed out sentences that she could use on her social network page. She continued to change the words around to succinctly convey what would be needed to project her thoughts so that others would take notice.

She finally settled on the right words and went to her page to begin typing: *My 80-year-old childhood CASA/GAL advocate needs help. Hospitalized, with medical bills piling up. Please help.*

The next day, she posted a picture of Velma and told a little about her accident.

The following day, she posted another plea, this time for monetary funds, and shared her home address.

On Monday, the postman rang Tonja's doorbell and said he couldn't get all the mail into their mail box. She was astonished as he handed her a box full of envelopes. "Ma'am, is it your birthday? You got a lot of mail here."

"No, it's not my birthday. But, it is a day of celebration." She didn't feel the need to explain the meaning behind her statement.

It took her way over an hour to open and read the letters and cards. When she was finished she counted up the money and just say there shaking her head in disbelief. She counted it a second time and sure enough there was over forty-thousand dollars sitting on her table. Dozens of checks for hundreds of dollars from single donors amazed her. She sat for quite some time in shock as she stared at the stack of money and checks.

That evening, in the newspaper, an article about Tonja's championing for funds for Velma made front page news. Someone had contacted the newspaper after receiving Tonja's postings on her social network page and told of Velma Pearce's financial dilemma.

That evening after work, Stephen had read only the first paragraph of that newspaper article when the hair on the back of his neck stood up. "What? Everyone will surmise that Mother is like a homeless person. Who started all of this?"

He read further in the article and saw Tonja's name. "Marianne, where's the phone book?"

"It's over there on the bottom rack of the telephone stand, where it's always been."

He grabbed it up and thumbed through the white pages. His finger ran down the columns looking for Tonja's last name. He came across three people with the same last name, but only men's names were listed or just initials. He decided to start with the first one and continue from there.

The first two calls revealed nothing. When a man answered the phone on the third call, Stephen asked, "Is Tonja there?"

"Who's asking?"

"Stephen Pearce."

He handed the phone to Tonja and said, "This could be a prank call. If it is, hang up on the guy."

"Hello," she said, quite skeptical.

"Tonja, this is Stephen Pearce, Velma Pearce's son."

Before he could say another word, she interrupted him, joyfully saying, "Mr. Pearce how nice of you to call. I've been so worried about your mother. Is she all right?"

"Each day she seems to be getting a tiny bit better, but she is not able to recognize people.

"I'm calling about the article in tonight's newspaper that tells of a plea for money for my mother. I'm a little appalled at such a plan to get money from people."

"Oh, wait a minute, Mr. Pearce. Your mother was my advocate when I was a little girl. She saved my life by being there for me, when I had no one else to turn to. I've never had the opportunity to do anything for her to show her my gratitude that she was a supporter of my plight. I heard that the young boy who caused your mother's accident and his mother do not have insurance. I felt that it was a way to take care of both your mother's medical bills and save the young boy's mother from humiliation for not being able to pay up."

"I see. Forgive me if I sounded condescending. I do wish, though, that you had talked with one of our family members before beginning this financial plea."

"I'm sorry, Mr. Pearce, if I have offended you. That was not my intent. I would like to share with you how much money has come in to date. After opening all the mail today, there is forty thousand two-hundred and two dollars and fifty cents.

"How much?" asked Stephen. He sat dumbfounded.

Tonja repeated the number. "The fifty cents came from a child in one of the elementary schools here in Middleton. Isn't that sweet?"

"Sure is. I'm a middle school teacher."

"I know. Your mother told me? Mr. Pearce, you will be touched by the beautiful notes that go along with the money. Not only by the generosity of the people in this community, but also individuals in states all over the U.S. I would like to get all these cards, letters and money to you soon. How could we do that?"

"If you're going to be home in just a little while, my wife and I will drive over to your place. I guess I can find your address in the phone book."

"It's in the last paragraph of the newspaper article in tonight's paper."

"Okay. I guess I didn't get down that far before I misinterpreted your kind gesture. Let's say we'll be there in about thirty minutes."

"Looking forward to meeting you, Mr. Pearce."

Tonja hated to hang up the phone, because she knew her husband would begin grilling her. He was not an unkind man, but had a short fuse that would set him off, temporarily. He would calm down soon afterwards.

He did throw a fit when she finally got around to telling him about the financial appeal, and stomped off to what the young men today call the 'man-cave' - the 'rec room' to the older generation. Whenever he was upset or wired up he played pool. He was good at it, and challenged himself to a game that night to beat his last score.

Tonja's meeting with Stephen and Marianne went well, Stephen leaving with a grateful heart that his mother's friend had sought to be there for her.

Tonja's husband had sat in on the conversation between his wife and Stephen. He was then able to get a better understanding of his wife's interference in other people's business.

On the way home, Stephen suggested that they deposit the money in his mother's savings account. Tonja had assured him that more money would be coming in after people read the evening's paper.

"Marianne, I see the Hand of God in all of this."

"In all of what, Stephen?"

"All this money coming in. First, James made decisions without conferring with the family and then Tonja taking matters into her own hands. I guess I got mad at Tonja for the same reason I was angry with James - I wasn't allowed to be a part of their decision-making. Sounds selfish, huh? It looks like the one hand that brought a solution to this problem belongs to God.

"I hate it that James is so all-fired-up about hunting for the Ramirez family like they are hardened criminals."

"Between the six of us kids, we could have scraped together money to cover some of the medical bills, but then Mother would have felt indebted to us for that."

When Stephen walked into their home, he headed straight for the phone. "I'm going to call the family and let them know what has occurred over the past couple of days. I can hear Cassie and Sonja screaming for joy when they hear about the financial plea."

"Are you going to call James?"

"Not tonight."

The next day's mail brought in an abundance of money, so much that it overwhelmed Tonja.

Chapter 27

It was two days since Stephen had met Tonja or had any contact with her. He opted not to bother her every day with enquiries about the funds coming in to her. He would wait and allow her to contact him. Only Tonja was aware that the fund had now grown ten times as much as that first day.

He and Marianne had just left the hospital for home that late afternoon after visiting with his mother, and he said, "Mother seemed more alert today, don't you think?"

"Yes. Her eye movement seemed quicker and she used her left arm a whole lot more than last night."

Stephen quickly replied, "Sonja told me that when she was there earlier today that mother appeared to recognize her. I didn't see that happening when you and I were there. I don't want to get impatient waiting for her to return to the vibrant mother we all know, but it sure is hard not to."

The two had no sooner walked in the door than the phone rang. Marianne was the nearest to it and picked up the receiver. "Hello. Oh . . . hi, James. . . . Yes, he's right here. Just a moment." She handed the receiver to Stephen and went to the kitchen to begin fixing dinner.

"Hey, brother, how are you?"

"Never mind how I am, big brother. Do I have good news for you."

"I could handle some good news."

"Are you sitting down?"

"Well, no. Should I be?"

Salt in an Unsavory World

"Well, hold onto your hat, as you'll be screaming hallelujah when I get through telling you what we've found. My law-partner, Greg, flew to Mexico to look up the Ramirez family and he hit pay dirt. He found Jose Ramirez, the kid's dad, in a small town just south of Juarez. Seems that he's been in the drug business there for the past five years and came up with a gold mine. He's living in a fancy hacienda with servants and body guards galore. Greg paid one of the policemen in that town for information and security to make a visit to the guy's place. But, that hasn't taken place as yet, but he's planning to get to the guy one way or another."

"Hold it, James. Hold it, right there. We don't need that guy's money anymore."

"Whatta ya mean? Mother's bills have got to be paid."

"They will be."

"How?"

"Money has come in from everywhere, cities I've never heard of. To date, over forty thousand dollars is now sitting in Mother's savings account."

"So what? That may take care of her medical bills, but that family needs to have punitive damages thrown at them. That kid knocked Mother down and she deserves to have compensation paid to her for all the pain and suffering she has endured."

"Well, that's something Mother will have to agree to."

"No way, Stephen. Greg and a couple of his cohorts are just waiting for the right time to invade the premises of Jose Ramirez. Once Greg has communicated with me the timing of that raid, I'll meet him in El Paso for a one-on-one to discuss the details."

"James, that's all so unnecessary."

"Big brother, you and your righteous ways of thinking make me sick. This is a dog-eat-dog world and if we don't retaliate in this situation, we, as a family, become the dog that runs home with its tail between its legs."

"Maybe so. But, Mother needs to be consulted on this matter before you do anything crazy."

"Is she talking now?"

"No."

"See, one of us needs to take a stand for our mother and I guess because the rest of you are wimps, it falls on me."

"James, I appreciate you informing me of your tactics, but I believe our phone call needs to end. I'll talk to you later."

"Wimp!!"

Stephen slammed the receiver down on its cradle. He was shaking. "I can't believe how far off the mark James has traveled in these past few years."

"You talking to me?" asked Marianne, sticking her head around the corner from the kitchen.

"No. To myself."

"And?"

"I'll tell you in a few minutes. I'm going down to the basement to work on my boat. Call me when dinner's ready. I'll tell you about James' call then."

Stephen had purchased a boat from a doctor in town who wanted to upgrade to a larger boat. He was taking the time during the fall and winter months to refurbish it, preparing it for the coming boating season in the spring. He planned to retire in the next couple of years and he and Marianne were planning to do some boating.

He took off his suit jacket and placed in on a wooden stool and found a piece of sandpaper to begin the smoothing process. He wanted to take off the two layers of paint to get down to the original wood and then put on a fresh coat of paint. It was a tedious task, but one that he enjoyed in the evenings after a long day in the classroom filled with pre-teens.

His thoughts immediately went back to the phone call with his brother. *I can't believe James would go through with this. It's so dangerous. Those Mexican drug dealers are killers. That drug money is too important to them to have someone try to take it away. Lord, I pray that I don't have to read about my brother's demise in a newspaper or on TV. He needs to be stopped, but there's nothing I or my brothers and sisters can do to stop him. Please, dear Lord, stop him before it's too late.*

Velma's dinner tray was brought to her room and placed on the bedside table. Trisha had volunteered to be at the hospital each evening to feed her mother-in-law. She pressed the button to raise the head of the bed. All the while that Velma's body was changing positions, her eyes darted back and forth.

Trisha tucked a napkin under Velma's chin and began to feed her the broth, pushing the soup spoon down ever so slightly against her tongue to make her open her mouth wider. She spoon-fed the entire bowl of broth to her, wiping her chin with the napkin when some of it drizzled from her mouth. Next came the Jell-O. That seemed to be more difficult for Velma to manage as sometimes she would choke on it. Trisha gave her sips of tea from time to time and she could tell by Velma's eyes that she was enjoying her drink.

Hot tea was a favorite drink of Velma Pearce. She had collected beautiful tea pots from everywhere. She purchased some on trips to Canada, while others were gifts from friends and family on her birthday or Christmas. Her husband, George, had made a special cabinet with glass doors and lights inside to illuminate the display of beautiful tea pots.

A nurse came in to check on Velma and told Trisha that the doctor wanted Velma to be gotten up in the morning to use the bathroom. "Oh, that'll be so much nicer for her," said Trisha. "I know that having a catheter can become so uncomfortable."

"It'll be good for her in many ways. She needs to get some strength back in her body and that can only be accomplished if she's moving," said the nurse.

When the nurse had left the room, Trisha phoned Sonja to tell her of this latest news.

"Great!" said Sonja. "I'm glad I can be there for that event."

Chapter 28

James sat in his law office, pondering what was going on in Mexico. Greg had flown to El Paso two days earlier to set up his plan to get to Jose Ramirez in order to force him to fork over money for Velma's medical expenses. He had not heard a word from him. Greg had not divulged the full plan to James prior to his departure, but did tell him that he might have to join him to carry everything to its conclusion – in a safe productive manner – that is.

When that call did come, it was a complete surprise to James because of what Greg expected of him. He soon found himself on a plane leaving Portland and heading for El Paso, Texas. He would need to change planes in Dallas to one headed south to El Paso.

Greg said that everything was in place to go ahead with the plan. They would make their way onto the property of Jose Ramirez, hopefully without any opposition and/or gunfire. Then, he would do his best to get inside the house to talk one-on-one with Ramirez.

James tried several times on that last phone call to weasel out of making the trip, knowing full well that his presence there could not help or hinder the situation. Anyway, he was a lawyer not a detective. But Greg felt it was vital for James to be there in person.

"Greg, you'd better know what you're doing. I'm not there to play games," James had told him.

"I know. I know," was Greg's reply.

When he went home that night, he knew he dared not tell Wanda all the details, but just that he had to meet Greg in El Paso to finalize some matters regarding the money from Jose Ramirez. "The less she knows, the less she'll worry," he said to his paralegal as they left the office at the same time earlier that evening.

A lot of thoughts went through James' mind as he tried to relax on the flight to El Paso. *My family has no concept of what is right or wrong for our Mother. They'll see who's right when I return with a bundle of money that will afford her a good life.*

He closed his eyes and tried to sleep, but couldn't. *Greg had better have this situation nailed down by the time I get there. I've got to get back in Portland for the Smith trial.*

Tom, one of Greg's hired men met James at the El Paso International Airport. One look at him and James thought *I wouldn't want to cross this guy – as even if I did, I probably wouldn't live to tell about it.*

During Greg's last call to James, he told him to wear a tan pull-over shirt with khaki pants – it would blend in with the locale, which was nothing but dirt and underbrush for miles in each direction. Tom immediately recognized James by what he was wearing.

The two were driven in a large black SUV with very dark tinted windows. A six-inch-wide clear space in the tint ran across the middle of the front windshield giving the driver an unrestricted view of the road ahead. They crossed the border into Mexico and then drove through a small town and then about ten more miles.

What looked like Plexiglas separated the driver from the two sets of passenger seats behind him. James could only surmise that it was actually bullet-proof glass. He felt so incarcerated. He turned to Tom to ask a question, but when he saw the deep-furrowed lines in the man's forehead, he quickly turned back. *That scowl would frighten even a ferocious lion.*

After several minutes, the SUV made a turn and the roughness of the road told James they had left the asphalt and were now on a dirt road.

Tom said curtly, "Ramirez lives out this way."

"Oh," said James.

They rode along for a little while and then came to an abrupt stop. James squinted as he looked through the darkened windows to figure out where they might be. All he could see was scrub brush and cacti.

They just sat there; not a word was spoken. James didn't see anyone approach the car, but suddenly the door beside him opened. He gasped. *I really didn't want to get involved in this mess. All this clandestine action was the reason I sent Greg down here to take care of this matter. He enjoys this kind of action.*

James wasn't about to admit, even to himself, that fear had now entered the picture. His heart was pounding and he realized that sweat beads had formed on his forehead.

A Latino man with an over-sized, bushy mustache and dressed in ragged blue jeans and a blue jean shirt reached in and grabbed James' arm and said something in Spanish.

James looked over his shoulder at Tom, "What's he sayin'."

"Git out," said Tom.

"I'm goin'." He looked back at the Mexican, and said, "Take your hands off me." He pulled his arm away from the guy.

He straightened his shirt when he got out and stood beside the vehicle. As he looked around, it was becoming darker. The sun was sliding gently beyond the horizon, but he could still make out the landscape. Way off into the distance he could see the outline of some buildings, and wondered if they were the Ramirez ranch house and adjacent buildings.

Just then, the driver put the car in gear and drove off in a cloud of dust. James was left standing there with the blue-jeaned character and Tom. *Now what?* James wondered.

"We're gonna make our way over to that building and make it fast," said Tom. "Keep yur head low."

About one hundred yards away was an old wooden weather-beaten shed that looked like it had been there since the war between the U.S. and Mexico. "Okay. Lead the way."

"Need to watch for snakes."

Good heavens. What have I gotten myself into? James thought as he made his way toward the old shed. He ran, but watched every step ahead of him for snakes.

The Mexican opened the door to the shed and in its darkened interior, James heard, "Well, it's about time, partner," said Greg.

"What've you gotten me into?" asked James.

"No problem. It's as easy as fallin' off a horse."

"I'm not good at horseback ridin'."

"I'll direct the show and you just follow. The mail truck is due here in . . .," he paused to look at his watch . . .

"about five minutes. The driver already knows the plan – he's been paid well. He's old and had planned to quit his job soon, anyway. As you full well know the financing for this trip isn't coming out of the firm's pocket - but yours! The mailman should be able to live on your money for the rest of his life. Knowing full well that Ramirez will come looking for him he plans to flee tonight to El Paso, where his son lives."

"I know this'll cost me something, but it'll be worth it. Okay, so the mail truck is coming, then what?"

"We get into the enclosed back-end and he'll drive us onto the property. He makes that trip every other day onto that compound about this same time as it's his last stop of the day. No one has ever stopped him. With darkness coming on, we'll wait in the truck while the mailman makes small talk with the men on guard. He already has a plan to attract their attention away from the truck, so that we can sneak out the back door."

"You keep saying 'we'," said James.

"Not you. You're going to stay in the truck, unless . . ."

"Unless what?"

"Unless I need you."

"What does that mean?"

"Come on, James. Stop being a doubter. We've gone over this plan several times with the mailman. On his previous runs out to the ranch, he's played the scenario over in his mind many times until he's got it down pat."

"What happens when you reach the front door?"

"The mailman said it's always open. He knows, because when he has a package to deliver he knocks and opens the door and places the package on an inside hallway table. No one ever checks to see who came through the door, as he's already passed by the guards who know him."

"You make it sound so easy."

"It is. Trust me. Okay, I think I can hear the mail truck coming down the road." To Tom, he said, "Check and make sure it's him."

Tom peered out the window and said, "It's him. Let's go."

"Do you mean we have to go back across that snake-infested field, again?"

"Yup. Like I said, let's go!"

The four men made their way across the field with the sun barely casting an orange glow across the horizon. Unable to check for snakes, James just started to run toward the mail truck. He could only hope that they had crawled off to find a safe resting place for the night.

The truck stopped and the four men got into the back. Even before they could get the door closed, the driver took off.

"Here we go," said Greg. "Everyone knows the plan, so good luck."

Never in his life had James been so frightened. *What've I got myself into? This isn't what I had planned.* His heart was now pounding harder than ever.

The truck slowed and then came to a stop. The driver backed the truck up to the steps to the front door, as he had always done. He then rolled down the window and yelled something across the way to one of the guards, who smiled and waved. He got out and walked toward the guards and was gesturing with his hands as he spoke. Those in plain view gathered around him to talk.

Greg whispered to James, "You stay here in the truck. I've got a feelin' that with your skepticism you might very well botch the job. Just sit tight."

"You won't have to tell me that twice."

The Mexican had been sitting on his haunches, his hand on the door handle, ready to spring. Now, at Greg's command, he opened the door and slipped quietly to the ground – the others followed.

The Mexican knocked and carefully opened the door and all three men slipped into the hallway.

Just then a Mexican woman, wiping her hands on her long white apron that cascaded down over her plump body, came into the hallway from a doorway on the right. She was startled. "What are you doing here?" she said in Spanish.

"Señora, we've come to see Señor Ramirez," said the mustached Mexican in Spanish.

Her eyes widened and she whirled around and began to yell in a frantic tone, "Señor. Señor Ramirez."

A man in his late forties with very striking features stepped through the door into the hallway. "Señora, what is it?" he asked her in Spanish. He then became aware of the three men. He grew quite suspicious when he saw that two of them were white men, probably Americans. In English he said, "Who are you?"

"I've come about your son, Anthony."

"What about my son."

"He's in great trouble. He has put an older woman in the hospital due to his carelessness. She may not live. But in the meantime, her hospital bills are piling up. Your wife does not have the means to pay those bills and we've come to request your help in this matter."

"What do you want from me?"

"Money! Your son may go to prison if we are not able to convince the judge that it was an accident. If Anthony pays for the woman's medical bills, it will look better to the judge and hopefully sway his decision in your son's favor. The injured woman's son is a lawyer and he's agreed to fight for your son, but only if you're willing to hand over the money."

"How do I know you're telling me the truth?"

"We have the woman's son waiting in the truck for us. He has come all this way from the State of Washington in support of his mother. Please, Mr. Ramirez, if you love your son, we beg of you to provide the money."

"How much are you talking about?"

"Three hundred thousand dollars."

"What? No medical bills cost that much."

"They do now in the U. S. The old lady will need rehabilitation if she gets out of the hospital. If she dies, well ... who knows what will happen to Anthony."

Jose Ramirez just stood there, not moving. Only his eyes and furrowed brow told the men that he was mulling over what he had heard.

Suddenly through the front door burst two men, handguns drawn. The three intruders backed up against the wall, not knowing what the guards were planning to do.

Jose spoke to them in Spanish and they holstered their weapons, but continued to stand in the doorway.

Soon, another guard came onto the porch and just ahead of him walked James with his hands in the air and a gun in his back. The guard shoved James into the hallway past the other two guards.

Just then, they heard the mail truck start down the road.

The guards, guns drawn, went to the door, but the mail truck was already too far down the road to be stopped.

Greg closed his eyes momentarily and contemplated the next move. He turned to Jose and said, "This is the woman's son, who is heartbroken over his mother's accident. As I told you before, he's a lawyer who is willing to help your son should he be arrested."

James looked at Greg, his mouth open in shock. *He's got to be crazy. I would've trusted Greg with my life. But now it seems I am horribly wrong. He'd use me no matter what the outcome would be.*

Jose again stood there, not speaking. Then he looked at James and said, "How do I know you'll do what this man has said."

Pulling out his wallet, James showed him his business card to verify that he was really a lawyer. Next, he thumbed through the plastic photo holder in his wallet to find the picture of his mother. Turning the picture toward Jose, he said, "This is my mother. She lives in Middleton, Washington where your wife and son live. I promise you that I will do all I can to help your son stay out of prison." He stepped back against the wall. *I can't believe I just promised to do that?*

Chapter 29

Back in Middleton, Velma's daily routine now consisted of a daily shower and using the bathroom. The catheter had been removed and she was now eating regular food. She would move the next day to a rehabilitation center for a week or so and then to her home for in-home rehab care.

The evening meal tray had been removed and Stephen and Marianne were sitting at her bedside. "Mother, would you like to sit up in a chair for a few minutes?"

She only responded with a slight nod of her head. The doctor and family were pleased with the slow, but sure progress she was making.

"Great. Let me help you into your robe," said Marianne. "Stephen will help you out of bed." Before Velma's feet hit the floor, Marianne knelt down and helped her into some cute slippers, a gift that someone had knitted.

After some maneuvering, Stephen was able to get her on her feet and over to the large chair. She was no sooner seated than Pastor Simpson walked through the doorway. He smiled at Stephen and Marianne and said, "How's our girl doing today?"

"She seems to be improving each day. Tomorrow she goes over to Coastal Rehab," said Stephen.

"How long will she need to stay there?"

"Possibly a week. Then she can go home. She needs to be taught how to feed herself and other normal everyday functions."

"It's so good to see her in that chair."

A faint sound came from Velma. "What is it, Mother?"

She repeated it and Stephen asked, "Tell me again, Mother."

"Paaastor," was the feeble word that he could make out.

"Pastor, I believe she has recognized you and is saying 'Pastor'." Stephen drew a chair up beside Velma and said, "Pastor, why don't you come over here and talk with her. Let's see what happens."

Stephen and Marianne backed away and allowed the pastor to begin talking with Velma. She turned her head toward him and a smile came over her face.

Stephen put his arm around his wife and said, "I think she knows him. Honey, why don't we leave and let him be alone with her? Being here might be a distraction for her."

She nodded in agreement.

"Pastor Simpson, we're going to leave now. On our way out, I'll ask the nurse to come in and put Mother back to bed in just a few of minutes. Goodnight, now."

"Goodnight, you two." He then turned his attentions to Velma. He reached for her hand and held it as he talked to her.

"Velma, I'm resigning as the pastor. Next week is my last time to preach from that pulpit. Oh, how I wish you could be there to hear me. Your presence would give me the confidence I need to speak.

"I offered to fill in for the new pastor whenever I'm needed. Do you understand what I'm saying?"

Velma smiled.

"Velma, if you understand me, squeeze my hand." He so wanted her to respond to his request, but she didn't. So he repeated, "Velma, if you hear me, squeeze my hand." Nothing, but then he felt a slight pressure from her fingers against his hand. His eyes lit up. "You do understand me, don't you?"

She smiled.

Oh, dear Lord in Heaven, she knows me. I pray that you will continue this healing until she's herself again.

He talked with her awhile and at times she seemed to respond. Then the nurse came in and almost in a sing-song voice said, "Mrs. Pearce, it's time to get back in bed."

"I believe she's tired, now," said Pastor Simpson, as he prepared to leave. "Velma, goodbye, my dear. I'll see you tomorrow." Peter Simpson's heart skipped a beat as Velma smiled back at him. He leaned over and gave her a kiss on the cheek.

The drive home was joyful and he couldn't help but begin to hum, in his own humble way, one of his all-time favorite songs, *Amazing Grace.* He loved music and he once quipped, "God blessed me with a voice to speak for Him, but not to sing. I can't hold a tune in a bushel basket."

When he reached home, he just had to tell someone the good news, so he called his sister, Nellie. They rejoiced together over this wonderful turn of events.

Chapter 30

Jose Ramirez ordered the four intruders into his living room. Out of the corner of his eye, James caught Jose whispering to his two cohorts, with one going into another room and the other out the front door.

The two lawyers were transfixed after entering the gigantic room and saw the luxurious furnishings. They were both used to fine furniture in their own homes and those of their friends, but nothing like this. They sat down on an enormous leather sofa, probably ten feet long, which sat across from three, huge leather armchairs. An ottoman was positioned in the middle of that setting, the size of a child's plastic swimming pool. Several people could easily be seated on it at one time. The two elaborate chandeliers that hung overhead and the large rock fireplace with logs ablaze were eye-catching adornments for that room.

Both lawyers realized that Jose brought them in there as a stall tactic. They surmised that he had not decided on what to do with the four intruders. He needed time to think.

Jose snapped his fingers and a servant leaned over his shoulder as he whispered to him. The man left the room and soon returned with a tray holding several wine goblets and set it down on that footstool. He then went over to a beautiful wood side-table and retrieved a bottle of wine.

"Gentlemen, how about a glass of wine?"

"Sounds good to me," answered Greg.

The servant poured the wine and then handed a goblet to each man, beginning with Jose.

Jose leaned forward to retrieve a cigar from a beautiful jeweled humidor and then offered one to each of the intruders. He clicked his fingers and immediately the servant reached for the cigarette lighter from where it sat beside the humidor and lit the cigar for his master.

The portly woman that they had first met appeared with an inlaid wooden tray with plates piled with cheese and fruit. She also set it down on the footstool.

James began to question Jose's generosity. *He's stalling and about to pull a rabbit out of a hat. I hate the thoughts of what he's gonna do next.*

The tone and the atmosphere had changed since their entry into the house. A fire in the fireplace and the wine began to make the intruders relax. Jose made small talk, asking about the men and their families.

Stay focused, James. He sent his two cronies out to do something. But what? He's up to something. I sure hope Greg doesn't let that wine go to his head. In the past, he could consume a lot before he became tipsy. I hope that's the case tonight.

One of Jose's partners who had earlier gone into another room, came back and now stood in the entryway to the living room. He cleared his throat and when Jose looked over at him, he nodded his head as if to say, 'come here'.

Jose got up and the two walked a few feet away to talk. James and Greg could only sit and speculate as to what they might be saying.

Then suddenly gunfire could be heard outside and everyone in the room stopped in their tracks. Jose walked to the side of a window and peered around the corner to take a look. "They must've been shootin' at some varmint on the property that was attacking our livestock."

A bullet came zinging through the window and everyone quickly ducked behind one of those oversized pieces of furniture. "What's goin' on?" asked Greg.

"Not sure," responded Jose.

Another volley of shots came through one of the other windows. Jose yelled out, "Everyone get out of here. Follow me." He led the four intruders to an inside room with no windows. He said, "Stay here. I'll be right back," and turned and left the room, closing the door behind him. They heard a key turn in the lock and they knew they had been locked in, with no way out.

More gunfire was heard, more than before.

"Somethin's goin' on, James, and I don't like the sounds of it."

"Me, either. But, what are we gonna do about it?"

They both turned to their Mexican partner and Greg asked, "Any suggestions?"

"Sounds to me like Señor Ramirez's enemies are getting revenge on him. It could get real bad. We must escape."

"But how?" asked James.

"There are four of us. We should have enough weight among all of us to knock that door down," suggested Tom.

"Sounds like a good idea. Without any other suggestions, let's do it," said James.

All four stood shoulder-to-shoulder in front of that massive door and Tom began to count "one, two, three - charge."

The four hit the door with everything they had, but it didn't budge.

"Again," said Tom.

They rushed the door again, but to no avail. They were shocked when it did not budge.

"Wait! Wait!" said James. "Boy, are we blind or what? Take a look at that door, fellas. It swings in and not out. We could've charged that door all day long, but nothing would've helped.

"We could take the hinges off the door," Tom suggested.

"Yeah, I guess we could. But, we'll need a screwdriver."

"Hey, fellas. Got one right here," said James, pulling the knife out of his pants pocket. My wife gave me this expensive pocket knife for my birthday and I've never used it. Just carry it around. I'd be mighty proud, fellas, if we'd use it now. Then if Wanda ever asked me if I liked the knife, I wouldn't have to lie to her."

That brought a smile from everyone.

Two of them worked to undo the pins holding the hinges. "There's the first one," said Tom. "Now let's get this second off and we're outa here."

"Hurry!" said Greg.

"I am," Tom hissed back.

The heavy door came loose and the men laid it down, while the others scrambled out.

"Which way do we go?" asked the Mexican.

"Your guess is as good as mine. Just lead the way," said Tom.

The four rushed down the long hallway in the direction away from the living room. James continued to look over his shoulder to make sure they weren't being chased. They came to a room at the end, opened the door and saw across the room a whole row of windows, and to their delight, an outside door right next to the last window.

Greg opened the door and slowly stuck his head out to and looked to see if he could see anyone. Not seeing a soul, one at a time, they slipped out the door and ran to the building that stood behind the house. They were able to breathe a sigh of relief when all four were safely behind that shed.

"Where do we go from here?" James asked, as he looked from one man to another.

Tom spoke up, "Um . . . Greg, when you asked me to stake out this place, I snooped around. This building here is at the back of the property. The shots seem to be coming from over there," he explained, pointing to his right. "So, I would say we go straight to our left for quite a spell and then turn right and hopefully it'll take us across the fields to the main road."

"Si, Amigo. I'm with you," said the Mexican.

"What other choice do we have?" asked James. "Let's go. You lead the way," he said to Tom.

The four started their escape with the Mexican bringing up the rear, watching over his shoulder every few feet. It wasn't without some mishaps, as one of them fell over a large stone. Another time, one of them ran smack into a cactus. "Ouch."

"Shh."

When they had moved quite a distance from the house, they decided to make that right-hand turn toward the main road. Tom reminded the others, "It's gonna be a long hike to that road, but that's our only chance of getting out of here."

"They're still shooting it out back there," said James.

"Yeah, I can hear 'em. I just hope they haven't discovered that we're missing or we'll have to make an even faster gallop for safety," said Greg.

"I'm almost out of breath," said James.

"Sorry, partner, but we've got to keep goin' or we'll be lyin' in a casket with our families boo-hooing over us," said Greg.

The four continued running, with gunfire sounding farther and farther away. Then they saw headlights and watched as a car came down the road from the ranch house. That could be their enemy or ours. We'd better lie flat on the ground until it's gone."

The only thought that went through James' mind at that moment was - snakes. Oh, dear Lord, why did I ever get started with this ordeal? I just wanted to set things right for my mother. I'm a lawyer, not a hoodlum.

"Hit the ground, men. A second vehicle just started down the drive from the house." As it got further down the road, they could see that it was a pickup.

For the next few minutes the four men kept their heads to the ground and their eyes peering to their right as they watched that second vehicle make its way to the main road.

All James could think about was the snakes, but also the tarantulas that the Mexican had talked about in the mail truck on their way to the Ramirez compound. He had told them that the Mexican tarantula is large and has a dark-colored body with orange patches and is deadly. "If you stand still, it will crawl up your shoe and then your leg," said the Mexican in his broken English. James shuddered at the thought.

"Hey, fellas, those vehicles may be gone, but the Ramirez gang is probably out here huntin' for us. Let's make a run for it," suggested Tom. "I watched as that last pickup made the turn onto the main road, and we don't have that much farther to go before we get to it."

"Then what?" asked James.

"Not sure," said Tom. "Let's get to the road first and then we'll decide."

James' legs ached, his lungs stung with pain from all the running. *I gotta keep going. There's no stopping now.*

"Where's that stupid road, anyway?" asked Greg.

"We should be hitting it any time now," said Tom. "Sure wished a car would go down that road so we can see just how far we still need to travel."

They kept running.

"These two-hundred-dollar shoes I'm wearing are worthless out here on this prairie," whispered James to Greg, as he came up beside him. "The rattlesnakes, lizards and tarantulas aren't at all impressed with these highly polished shoes, and I know those two guys with us could care less. Wish I was wearing my old beat-up Nikes. They don't look so hot, but they're comfortable."

"James, you beat all. Talking about shoes, when our life is on the line."

"Greg, don't you get it. You and I have spent years out there in the world, trying to impress people with our grand apparel - and those same individuals are doing their best to impress us. Whether we are wearing a pair of eighteen-hundred dollar Berluti's or a hundred-dollar Nike sport shoe, it doesn't make you or me a better lawyer, nor do those fancy shoes help us to run faster."

"James Pearce, I thought I knew you, but at this very moment, I don't really understand you at all. Here we are running from drug dealers to save our hide and you're philosophizing over who we are to a pair of shoes? I don't get you, man."

"Guess it's 'cuz I've never before been at the mercy of someone holding a gun in my back," responded James.

"Well, Dr. Sigmund Freud, we'd better run a little faster or we'll end up six feet under."

Tom ran back to the pair and said, "Come on, fellas. You'd better get a move on, or you'll be a notch on the barrel of Jose Ramirez's gun."

"Let's go, Greg," said James. "I'll race ya to the road."

As they ran, James thought about Greg and his dare-devil, James Bond-style approach to life. *He's always trying to prove something to others as well as to himself. But, I guess if I did a check of myself, I'd find that I'm no better than he is. Look where I am at this moment -- running from a drug lord. Heaven help me!*

Chapter 31

Sonja busied herself arranging her mother's breakfast tray so that it was easier for her to reach each of the side dishes. This had become her morning ritual once Velma began to sit up and eat regular food.

"Thank you," said Velma.

Shocked, Sonja almost dropped the lid to the main dish. "What did you say, Mama?"

"Thank you."

Sonja reached around the tray to hug her mother. "You're talking. Mama, you're talking."

Velma nodded her head.

"Did you know that you'll be leaving here today and going over to Coastal Rehab?"

Velma nodded her head.

Sonja just stood there with her mouth gaping open.

"Who are you?"

"Velllllma," she replied.

"Oh, Mama, I can't believe you're actually conversing with me. Who am I?"

Velma squinted and tilted her head back and forth and then said, "My baaaaby Son . . . ja."

"Well, you'd better get busy and eat. You're going for a ride over to the rehab center. I brought you your favorite outfit, in case you meet some handsome gentlemen over there."

Her mother smiled.

Sonja's heart was rejoicing. She wanted to drop everything she was doing to call her family and share the news, but it would have to wait. Her mother would be transferred at nine o'clock and she still needed to have a shower, get dressed and have her hair combed.

The bedside phone rang and Sonja picked it up.

"This is James Pearce. May I speak to one of Mrs. Pearce's family members?"

"James, this is Sonja."

"Oh. Hey, girl, how are you?"

"James?"

"Yes."

"James Pearce?"

"Yes, silly."

"You don't sound like yourself."

"If the truth be told, I'm more myself today than I have been in a long while."

"What are you saying?"

"I'll explain later. I just wanted to know how Mother is today."

"She's being transferred to Coastal Rehab in about an hour. She's carrying on a conversation now. Not long sentences, but she knows who we are and she knows who she is."

"Great news. I just wanted you to know I'm driving up there this weekend. I'll get there sometime around dinner time Friday. I need to talk to all of you."

Sonja gulped and her eyes rolled up. *Oh, no. He's gonna start that business about getting money from Mrs. Ramirez's family.* "Well, James, we'll be here."

"Good. I'll call you on my cell when I get closer to Middleton. I'd like to meet with all of you there in some restaurant and then call the out-of-towners on a conference call so that you can all hear me out."

"Whatever you say, James."

"Now, I'd like to say hi to Mom."

"Sure." Sonja held the phone receiver to her mother's ear. "Mama, James is on the phone."

Velma's eyes lit up.

"Hi, Mother," said James.

At first Velma did not answer him and her eyes were moving in all directions. Then a smile formed.

"Mother, this is James."

"Helllllo," said Velma.

"Mother, it's so good to hear your voice."

"Thank you." Velma grabbed the receiver and handed it to Sonja. "James."

"Yes, Mama, that was James . . . James, I wish you could see her eyes. They are literally dancing. She knew who you were."

"Great. Okay, sis, I'll see you on Friday."

James' call left Sonja with different feelings. *Guess I'll have to do some prayin' to ask the good Lord to help me hold my tongue on Friday while James spews out his attack on the Ramirez family. But, right now I need to get Mama ready to be transferred at nine.*

Later that evening, Sonja called her siblings and conveyed to them James' message about Friday. They, too, were just as skeptical about his intentions. They knew nothing of his escapades to Mexico and could only assume that he would be laying out a grandiose plan by which money could be extorted from Anthony's father.

During the past week, Tony and his mother had visited Velma, but she was not told that he was the young boy on the bicycle who knocked her down. That information would wait until she was much more in control of her mind. He happened to be just one more young person to visit her in the hospital.

On the first visit, Tony and Consuela were picked up by Sgt. Jackson and his wife Connie and brought to the hospital. The meeting between Connie and Tony went well.

On the second visit, Connie and Tony took the bus and made it a special time when they stopped off downtown to their favorite pizza place. Consuela had spent very little 'quality' time with her son, due to her work schedule. She had discovered during the events of the past few weeks that her son needed more attention than she had been giving him since his dad departed.

She had discussed with him and encouraged him to enroll in the after-school wrestling program. He needed time with other males who could provide a good example for him. She knew the wrestling coach, who volunteered for that program each afternoon, as he was a good customer at the convenience store where she worked. One day she had the opportunity to talk to him about her son.

Even though Sgt. Jackson had encouraged Tony not to worry about the fall-out from Mrs. Pearce's accident, he still would wake up in a cold sweat at night from nightmares about the day that he hit her with his bike.

Consuela told her priest about those episodes and he had a long talk with the boy, trying to help him to put down fear and embrace the love and mercy of God.

The visits to Velma helped in that respect. The more he was around the elderly lady and saw the progress that she had made since his previous visit, the less he was afraid of her dying. Death had meant a lifetime sentence in prison for him.

≈

Velma's move to the rehab center was uneventful. She was placed in a room with a roommate, a very talkative roomie. Later, her family would come to realize that the lady, who asked a lot of questions, was good for their mother, as Velma had begun to answer her.

Chapter 32

Gordon and Trisha, Stephen and Marianne, along with Sonja and Jeff, had already arrived at the restaurant that Friday evening and were now awaiting James to show up. When he called earlier from his cell phone, Sonja let him know that they would meet him at LaCosta Mexican Restaurant. They had no idea that James had traveled to Mexico or the escapades that he had endured there.

James shuddered when she said Mexican, but knew better than to refuse to meet them there.

When he drove up in front of the restaurant, Stephen whispered, "Here comes trouble now."

"Yeah, in his torch-red Corvette coupe." said Gordon.

"Stop drooling, honey," said his wife, with a grin. He knew what she meant.

The family had decided that even though they had issues with him about the money, they planned to first wait and hear him out. He sat down and the family made small talk at the beginning, almost like a stall tactic on both sides. They really didn't want to hear what he had to say to them and he was reluctant to begin what he must say.

After the main course and while enjoying their desserts, James spoke up. "I'd like to place the conference call to Cassie and Paul now. That is if I can remember how to do it on this new-fangled cell phone I just got." He had never been as nervous as he was at that moment. While in his car, he had rehearsed over and over again what he wanted and needed to say.

James fumbled around with the cell phone and with Stephen's help, the two finally figured out how to make the conference call. They put the phone on 'loudspeaker' and placed it in the middle of the long, rectangular table where they were sitting.

"Cassie, is that you?

"Yes."

"Paul are you there?"

"Yup."

"Great. I'm here with the rest of the family, except that Wanda couldn't make the trip. Um . . . I guess first of all I want to apologize to all of you for being a jerk the last time we were together."

As he talked, the family members were awestruck at his words. Stephen's eyes darted back and forth from his wife to Sonja and then to Gordon. *Is this James Pearce, our brother?*

Then he began to share with them that he had made a trip to Mexico. From time to time he looked squarely into the face of a family member, but most of the time he looked down at his plate. They all listened intently as he told of the confrontation at the Ramirez ranch and their escape from the clutches of possible death. His story seemed right out of the pages of a John Grisham novel - a lawyer caught up in a grueling situation with a drug kingpin.

When he paused for a moment, Cassie said, "James, can you hear me?"

"Yes."

"You told us about escaping from the house, but how did you get back to civilization without being spotted by Ramirez's henchmen?"

"Cassie, that was the worst night of my life. You might laugh, but while we were running through a snake-infested area, my whole life passed before me . . . like a video. My shoes were killing me, my heart was pounding and my lungs hurt so bad that it was hard to take a deep breath.

"We got to the main road, but then decided that we were sitting ducks for Ramirez's goons if we stayed on the road. So we crossed the road and ran along the deep ditch that was dug out on both sides of the road. We figured that whenever we saw the lights or heard a vehicle coming we would lie flat in that ditch. Many times I stubbed my toe on a rock or some other object that I couldn't see, but kept on running.

"I could just imagine a snake or some other varmint attacking me while I was lying there in that ditch, but thankfully we did not have to prostrate ourselves the whole way back to town."

That explanation brought a chuckle from his family, as they looked from one to another.

"It's funny now, Cassie, but at the time I knew that my degrees, my law practice, my status in the Portland community could not help me. Only God could!"

Sonja caught herself gasping with surprise, but also delight. She shut her mouth quickly.

"It was a long, long ways back to town. After more than an hour of walking, we could see in the distance a faint light coming from a house or building. We knew we were getting close."

The family was silent. They seemed in agreement not to interrupt their brother again.

"I had already taken off my two-hundred-dollar pair of shoes and finished the trip in stocking feet, as those shoes had been hurting me something awful. At one point, I wanted to just heave them into the field alongside of the road. But, I didn't have another pair to wear back to Portland, so I tied the shoes by the shoestrings around my belt and let the shoes dangle there the rest of the way.

"Since Tom had arrived in that little village some six days earlier, we followed him and his directions the rest of the way there. It was probably ten or eleven o'clock by then, we really didn't know, as I had left my Rolex in my suitcase while in the back of that mail truck. I didn't want to allow Ramirez's cohorts or guards to steal it from of me.

"Either the mailman or someone else is now toting my two-thousand-dollar watch on his arm. I guess I'll be stopping by WalMart to pick me up a Timex – they're just as good, and as they've been advertised for decades – it'll take a licking, but goes right on ticking."

Everyone laughed and Cassie was overjoyed to once again hear his humor return.

"The whole fiasco ended when we got to the hotel where Tom had been staying. The Mexican fella left us there at the front door and he went on home.

"The hotel was a tiny rinky-dink place and Tom knew there probably wasn't another room available. We also didn't want anyone in town to see us and give away our location to the Ramirez gang.

"Tom went in and while asking for his key, he distracted the night manager's attention away from the front door. We then slipped in and up the stairs to his room. There was only one bed for the three of us, so the other two slept on the bed and I got the chair. Even though it was mighty uncomfortable, I fell asleep and didn't wake up until the sun came streaming through the window onto my face.

"The rest of the story is very uneventful. Greg and I spent hours at the airport, trying to get a plane home. Getting to the airport at the last minute, we weren't able to get on the same plane. I was pleased because I wanted to be by myself. I had a lot of thinking to do.

"As the plane headed for Dallas, I sat there in my seat and recalled what I had just gone through the night before. I snickered when I said to myself, *I'll never look at snakeskin shoes or anything else made from their skin with the same admiration as before – never, ever again."*

His listeners smiled.

"Then I took on a more serious tone. My question to myself was, 'What did you accomplish through all of this?' Nothing - was my only answer.

"Greg used me as a bargaining chip, knowing full well that I or any one of us could have gotten killed in the midst of it all. The whole situation could have turned a hundred-eighty degrees and I would have been taken as a hostage. It's very difficult for me now to even consider Greg as my law partner. He was only thinking of himself. He craves the adrenalin rush he gets when he's in a dangerous or precarious situation."

James paused, looked down and then lifted his head to look at his siblings. "Sitting there on that plane, I was appalled when I thought of how Mother would have reacted to my taking matters into my own hands instead of leaving it up to God. I'm so glad she doesn't know what an utter fool I was - and all the time I thought I was doing it for her.

"I have insulted you - my family, degraded my profession and humiliated myself to my wife and my office staff.

"I have lowered myself in the eyes of anyone who had ever respected me." He paused again. "I plan to sell my part of the law practice. Only time will tell as to when that will take place.

"That's it, family. Your brother has made a complete fool of himself. I apologize and ask that you forgive me for trying to control the family and to undermine our mother's Christian principles." With those words, he lowered his head and expelled a big sigh of relief.

Sonja reached across the table and with tears in her eyes, she laid her hand on his. "James, you are so forgiven."

Gordon spoke up, "I believe I can speak for the whole family, James, when I say that no one in the Pearce family will ever divulge to Mother about your trip to Mexico or the reason for it." The family all nodded in agreement.

James was so overwhelmed to speak.

Cassie couldn't say anything either as she was crying so hard that Bob had to speak for her. "James, this is Bob. Cassie is overcome by your humble apology and she forgives you and she's nodding her head in agreement. Cassie had told me over the past several years, 'That's not my brother. He wouldn't act like that.' James, she now has her brother back and I know she is very thankful for that."

After all the goodbyes had been said, James pushed the 'off' button on his cell phone and just sat there. One by one his brothers, sister and in-laws got up and hugged their baby brother. It was every evident to everyone that his stature had grown by leaps and bounds right before their eyes. The prodigal son had come home, and they were now a whole family - once again.

Epilogue

Velma's medical bills from rehabilitation and the hospital had piled up, but in time they were completely paid for with the abundance of funds that had come in to Tonja. The fund had eventually grown by another twenty-five-thousand dollars. The monies left over provided for a caregiver for Velma until she could be completely on her feet.

She had progressed steadily during her ten days at the rehab facility. She had learned to feed herself and with some help she managed to dress herself. She now recognized people and could carry on a dialog with them - in short sentences. At times memory lapses would cause her short gaps in her conversations. The doctor's prognosis for Velma was positive. He believed that she would fully recover.

She had daily visits from her best friend, Peter Simpson - now retired. The hardest part about his time with her was that she couldn't remember to call him Peter instead of Pastor Simpson. He would then reassure her that old habits die slowly.

They would sit and listen to music or he would read to her from a book of her choice, and always from the Bible. When spring came, they sat on the back veranda of Velma's home in those canary-yellow Adirondack chairs to watch the beautiful sunsets that sent hues of yellows and oranges across the horizon. Peter had commented to her once, "It's as though our Lord has taken His finger and painted that picture on the canvas of life just for you and me."

Velma couldn't wait to get back into church and this time she would no longer take the bus, but would be chauffeur-driven – by Peter. He had already informed her that she would have her choice of where they would stop to eat Sunday dinner on the way to take her home. Those future plans helped her to set a goal to be completely well by summer.

Peter still missed studying for the preparation of messages for services at the church and the interaction with people in the congregation. But, he was finding that the slower pace agreed with him. At first, he was antsy, feeling unfulfilled and sometimes even useless as he puttered around his house. He often found himself meandering through his house, looking for what – he didn't know. But, in time he did find other outlets besides the many hours each day he spent with Velma at her home.

For James and Wanda, it took some time before he could convince his wife that the big life in Portland was no longer a priority for him. He wanted to set up a practice in a smaller town, one that could use a good lawyer. He wanted to fit into a community where they both could be productive.

He had a couple of different cities in mind, but he kept them to himself until he felt that Wanda was on the same page with him. She had not experienced a stopping-point in her fast-paced life, such as the one that he had encountered in Mexico. He was well aware of that and would be patient until her eyes were opened to the real world instead of the highfalutin, pretentious world they had been living in.

James had also become aware of the prejudice he had exhibited toward Mexicans and other ethnic groups. He realized that he had truly convinced himself that his opinion of them was justified. It took some time to overcome those judgments, as they were pretty deeply ingrained within him over the past fifteen or so years.

The other members of the family went on with their lives, grateful to God for Grace and Mercy in His intervention in their mother's healing process and financial situation.

They were also very grateful to God for their brother's change of heart. They were all well aware that only God knows a person intimately enough to decide when an individual will respond to a red flag waved in their face. Only He knows, if and when, that would take place. The six children and their spouses spent a joyous Christmas that year with Velma in her home. Peter Simpson was happy to be included in that celebration.

While Velma was still in the hospital, Stephen had called and talked with Consuela about any visits that she and Tony would make to see his mother. He suggested that no mention be made to her of the fact that he was the boy on the bicycle. "She's still not ready to hear that right now. Let's let her get to know Tony first," he told Consuela. He also put her mind at ease about his mother's hospital bills, sharing with her how the money came in from people who had never met Velma, but who had big hearts.

After James returned from Mexico, Stephen went to the police station to share with Sgt. Jackson what he had learned about Jose Ramirez. With that information, Sgt. Jackson phoned Consuela, advising her to have a restraining order placed against her husband. She and her son needed that type of protection.

Tony did take wrestling classes after school and trained hard so as to try to earn a place at the top, but came in second in his division. That only motivated him to strive harder for first place. His mother said that if his grades ever began to fall, he would have to drop that after-school activity - immediately.

As for Consuela, she continued with her job at the convenience store, saving up as much money as possible to send Tony to college.

Months later, she received a letter from Jose, which demanded that Anthony come to live with him. If she refused, she could expect retaliation. The concept of her son living with his father in that unsafe world of drugs was more than she could stand. She took the letter to Sgt. Jackson at the police station, seeking his advice. With that letter and after hearing from Stephen Pearce about the encounter that his brother had with Jose in Mexico, a bench warrant was then issued for his arrest. Should he ever be spotted in the area or anywhere near her home, he would be arrested. Sgt. Jackson asked Consuela to keep him up-to-date on any further communication she might have with her husband.

Consuela requested that the landlord change the lock on her front door, in case Jose still had a key. Sgt. Jackson had also advised Consuela to get a divorce and ask for full custody of her son.

As for Samantha, she would continue to stay on with Catherine and John Williams, an arrangement that seemed to have been made by God.

Connie Jackson continued with her work as a child advocate with the CASA/GAL program. She visited Velma on a regular basis and even took her mentor out for lunch from time to time after Velma had become stronger.

≈

It was now months since Velma was thrown into utter darkness on that dreary, rainy day. It had taken that much time for therapy to return her to some semblance of a normal life.

On a bright and sunny afternoon in late May, Velma and Peter leisurely walked around her yard, viewing the beautiful flower beds that bordered the back of the house. She held tightly to his arm, as she was still unsteady whenever she was on her feet.

She heard the screen door open and turned to see who it was. The care-giver had come out to announce that Velma had company.

The screen door opened again and out stepped Stephen, followed by Tony and Consuela Ramirez. Seeing them was a welcome surprise for Velma. After their greetings, Stephen asked his mother if they could all sit down, as he had some news to share with her.

It was a tense moment for Tony and Consuela, but Stephen did most of the talking. He would share, for the first time, the details of the accident that took place between Tony and Velma. The family had only shared bits and pieces with her before this.

When Stephen had finished, Velma looked at Tony and then at Consuela, both had their heads bowed and were staring down at the floor. They raised their eyes to meet Velma's when she spoke. "About a month before . . . before . . . ah . . . the accident I had a dream." She stopped and then smiled. "It wasn't because I ah . . . ate too many beans, either." Everyone smiled.

Her demeanor then changed to a pensive as she looked upward. "In that dream I was . . . um . . . looking down on a scene that included me as I waited on a street corner." She stopped for a moment and the others anxiously waited until she was ready to continue.

Then she turned to look right at Tony. "Tony, as I stood there I heard ah . . . ah . . . a voice that said, 'Do not despise new beginnings . . . Velma . . . for your life is about to change.' Then I woke up. I pondered on those words time and again, as . . . um . . . as to what the dream implied. When I asked God about it, I only heard silence. Thoughts of the dream . . . ah . . . came back while I was in the hospital and again . . . ah . . . at the rehab center. I didn't understand it's meaning until just now.

"Come over here, son, and sit by me." She patted the small footstool that sat beside her chair.

Tony reluctantly rose and walked over to sit down.

She slowly took hold of his hands and looking deep into his bewildered face, said, "Tony, I want you to know that I had already been scheduled for . . . ah . . . um . . . a hip operation that was to take place three weeks from that day of the accident. But . . . Tony, that procedure was taken care of during my hospital stay. So, you see everything works for good. Please, never feel guilty again over . . . um

... ah ... the accident that took place. Our God knew that it was going to happen and has resulted in new experiences ... in my life and ... ah ... I hope, in yours. And ... you know what, Tony? I ... ah ... would never have met you and your mother." She smiled at him. "That has been a real blessing. I learned a long time ago, that ... that ... God has a plan for each of our lives, and He's ... ah ... He's always there to see us through that plan."

Tony did not smile back, but looked directly into her face and said, "Mrs. Pearce, when you were lying on the ground that day, I kept asking you to forgive me. I hope you know that I would never have hurt you on purpose. Please believe me!"

"Oh, Tony, I do. I know you wouldn't hurt anyone. And ... ah ... I do forgive you. I believe that the good Lord has a plan for your life and ... if you'll obey and follow His directions, He's going to take you into ... ." She hesitated, and as she regained her thoughts, she continued. Without any hesitations between words, she said, "He has a plan for your life, Tony. Obey Him and follow His directions and you'll go far."

Tony smiled. He was quite relieved that this woman who had suffered so much at his hands would forgive him. He leaned over and gave her a hug.

"I love you, Tony," she whispered in his ear, "and so does Jesus. Never, ever forget that."

"Yes, ma'am."

Stephen sat there thinking, *wished Sgt. Jackson could have been a part of this scene today to watch the interaction between Tony and my mother. As a teenager, Tony has learned a great lesson in life about love. We have truly witnessed a real love story here today.* With his thumb he wiped away the tears that had formed in his eyes.

Velma would love to have shared with those present that God's plan for her was also to include bringing Peter into her life, but she knew that was too personal to share. She did not want to embarrass Peter.

Velma Pearce would not return as a volunteer for the Court Appointed Special Advocate program. But, the outstanding role she exhibited as an advocate for young abused children lives on as an example for other volunteers to follow, which now includes Tonja.

It is impossible to know just how many individuals and children Velma Pearce had befriended over the years. Her co-workers, friends at church, neighbors and family members would tell you that the love and compassion she shows forth toward others is her trademark. She has made and continues to make a difference - for the better - in almost every life that she touches.

Velma is truly *salt in an unsavory world.*

About the Author

Author, freelance writer and speaker, Janet Nicolet, resides in the panhandle of Florida. She retired at age sixty-nine in 2005 as an administrative assistant. Within a year, she began writing – something very new for her.

In 2006, she authored her personal memoir titled "Vintage Years, *A Fulfilling Life after Divorce*". From 2007 to 2009, she undertook a new project - a *novel* trilogy. They are titled, "Kerri", and are based on the lives of her four adult children. She tackled a different genre in 2010, when she wrote a historical *novel*, "Long Journey Westward", which depicts a family's emigration from Ireland to Canada in the late 1880s.

"I Was There" was written in 2011. Military memories were recaptured and told to her by the men and women residents at the C.C. Sims Veterans' Nursing Home near Panama City, Florida.

Later that year she authored the fictional book, "Scooterville", filled with whimsical and also warm and fuzzy stories that depict senior living in a seniors' apartment complex.

She has taught memoir writing at senior centers in her area and is now a part of the cast of a local television talk-show titled "Seniors for Seniors".

The author's books may be reviewed and purchased on her website, www.myvintageyears.com or at on-line bookstores, which are also in eBook format. You may contact her by email with comments or for information at janbythebay21@juno.com.